The Stress Solution

A Revolutionary New Method for Emotional Resilience

For Melinda
with love,
La

3.20.21

Laurel Mellin, PhD

EBT Books

Brain Based Health with the tools of Emotional Brain Training (EBT) is a science-based approach to health, using techniques based on neurophysiology and emotional neuroplasticity that are designed to promote stress resilience and raise the brain's set point. As with any skills training program, EBT is not without risk and may be unsafe or ineffective for some people. If you have any psychological or medical problems, consult with your physician and other health professionals before beginning this program. EBT is not medical care, but skills training used in support of improving preventive and therapeutic health outcomes. Certified EBT Providers and Coaches are licensed, certified, or registered health professionals, educators, and first responders who facilitate EBT services and are providing services outside their professional licensure. Use of the Brain Based Health by EBT mobile app and participation in coaching and small group training facilitated by Certified EBT Professionals are recommended. The health outcomes associated with self-study use of EBT are not known. The author, The Solution Foundation (a non-profit corporation), and EBT, Inc. (a California corporation) disclaim all liability for any adverse effects that may result from the use or application of the information contained in this book. The characters discussed in this publication are composites of several individuals, and the names of all individuals have been changed to maintain anonymity. *Strong language appears in this book to provide greater authenticity regarding processing emotions in states of stress overload. Parental caution is suggested.* For more information about the science of EBT and research on program effectiveness, please visit www.ebtconnect.net/science.

Editors: Frannie Wilson and Michele Welling. InDesign production: Jamie Holecek. Graphics design: Steven Isakson. Graphics consultant: Jami Spittler. Production: Michael McClure. Technology: Dev Singh and Andrea Singh. Technology design: Joe Mellin. Creative advisor: Walt Rose. Manager: Kelly McGrath.

ISBN: 978-1-893265-04-2
Author: Laurel Mellin, PhD
Published by: EBT Books, a division of EBT, Inc.
138 Woodland Avenue, San Anselmo, CA 94960
EBT website: www.ebt.org
Laurel's blog: www.brainbasedhealth.org
Professional certification: www.ebtgroups.org
Questions: support@ebt.org

For Walt,
who is my dream
come true

You may say I'm a dreamer
But I'm not the only one
I hope someday you'll join us
And the world will be as one

~ Imagine by John Lennon

Also by Laurel Mellin

What's My Number?

The Stress Overload Solution

The Stress Eating Solution

Spiral Up!

Wired for Joy

3-Day Solution Plan

The Pathway

The Solution

Contents

Introduction   I

Part I.
The Pandemic of Toxic Stress

1. What's Happening? It's Stress   1
2. The Stress Brain   9
3. Emotions and Stress   17
4. The Virus: Toxic Stress   37
5. The Antibody: Radical Resilience   49

Part II.
The Solution

6. The Stress Release   57
   - Minute #1: Talk About the Situation   63
   - Minute #2: Express Healthy Anger   67
   - Minute #3: Negative Emotions Become Positive   70
7. The Power Booster   75
   - Minute #4: Take Action With Purpose   80

Part III.
Radical Resilience

8. Sustain Your Immunity: The 7 Rewards   93
   - Reward #1: Sanctuary   101
   - Reward #2: Authenticity   108
   - Reward #3: Vibrancy   115
   - Reward #4: Integrity   119
   - Reward #5: Intimacy   127
   - Reward #6: Spirituality   132
   - Reward #7: Freedom   137
9. Keep it Simple: The 3 Rules   147
10. Imagine a World at One   159

Epilogue: A Revolution From Within 169

Appendices
    A Quick Guide 177
    More Support 179
    Next Step 183
    Glossary 187
    Selected Readings 191
    Acknowledgments 195

Introduction

In the early months of 2020, we were all confronted by the urgent need for a comprehensive response to a new strain of highly infective coronavirus. Our transactional lives were put on hold as everyone was tasked with negotiating social isolation vs. vulnerability to illness or loss of life. The resulting stress exacerbated the emotional overload of an already epidemic stress health crisis.

The World Health Organization has acknowledged the "hidden" epidemic of stress in modern life and the very real physical and emotional health crisis that results. Studies have identified the emotional brain as the "stress brain." By unleashing its power to release stress and activate positive emotions, we create a force field of well-being around us so that we can live in a stressed world without becoming stressed out.

As a health psychologist and stress researcher, I believe we need a vaccine for the coronavirus, but also a "vaccine" for stress, a way for all of us to become radically resilient – able to bounce back from stressful moments quickly and easily. The Covid vaccine is in development, but the stress vaccine is already here. It is Emotional Brain Training (EBT).

We need to reset our approach to stress to become radically resilient as our health is rapidly deteriorating. In April 2020, a study conducted by San Diego State University researchers of a representative sample of people in the US showed that 70 percent of participants met the criteria for moderate-to-serious mental distress, compared with only 22 percent in 2018. In June 2020, happiness plummeted to an all-time low in the US. Among adults under 25, roughly 90 percent screened positive for moderate-to-severe depression, and 80 percent screened positive for moderate-to-severe anxiety. During shelter-in-place, more people sought more psychoactive drugs, with an 11 percent increase in anti-anxiety meds and a 10 percent rise in antidepressant use compared to the year before.

What scared me was that this decided downturn in our quality of life came on top of decades of denial about our stress overload and the price we pay for side-stepping dealing with our stressed-out emotions. The old view of stress was that we were tense or upset. It was psychological. The emerging concept is that stress is physiological. The fight-or-flight response, cut loose from an ever-ready way to switch it off, activates a stress chemical cascade that promotes both emotional and physical health issues. It causes internal mayhem that brings on premature aging and wear and tear that increase our personal vulnerabilities.

These health issues range from annoyances like back pain or digestive issues to the diseases that cause premature death in adults: cancer, diabetes, and heart disease. In a study of primary care clinics, stress was a root cause of 75 to 90 percent of health concerns. More than 100 million adults in the US are now living with diabetes or prediabetes – fueled by stress directly and through the sugar cravings and weight gain these conditions cause – and 150 million adults nationwide are overweight or obese. One in seven of us meet the criteria for addiction. Deaths by suicide have increased by about 30 percent in the last 20 years, and work stress alone kills 120,000 Americans annually. We are hurting.

There was a time when we looked to medications to save us from what ails us, but innovations in drugs have been sorely lacking for 20 years. What's more, there are no medications that can control the emotional brain and make it radically resilient. Despite spending double what other wealthy countries pay per person on healthcare, including the highest per-capita pharmaceutical expense in the world, the US currently ranks last in life expectancy among the 12 wealthiest industrialized nations. The "a pill for every ill" approach failed. We need something more.

Sigmund Freud proposed some 140 years ago changing the emotional brain's pathways as a treatment for psychological and behavioral problems. Yet, sophisticated brain imaging equipment was not available at the time to prove his theory. Since then, neuroscientists have confirmed the existence of unconscious memories encoded in the brain, and brain science has shown that daily experiences can update these pathways. As these wires control our entire physiology, rewiring the emotional brain – positive emotional plasticity – offers a unifying approach to mental, behavioral, and physical health. It is a foundational strategy for potentiating the effectiveness of our healthcare.

Freud developed psychoanalytic approaches to changing the emotional brain, but they were so impractical and non-scalable that behaviorism began to take hold. Using direct approaches to change behavior through reinforcement and conditioning was appealing. However, it maneuvered around the emotional brain rather than changing it. As the emotional brain is the controller of our physiology, that may have been a factor in limiting behaviorism's effectiveness. Behavioral approaches have been highly effective in producing short-term changes of specific symptoms, but they have failed to generalize to other symptoms or produce lasting change.

With the emotional brain in stress largely untouched by behavioral therapies, faulty pathways in the emotional brain continue to fire, wire, and become stronger and fuel our epidemics of stress-induced problems. Behaviorism has evolved – it has had four waves: behavioral, cognitive, acceptance, and social/spiritual. Despite all our effort to fine-tune these methods, they have not been shown to rein in the stress overload of modern life.

EBT may prove to be the launch of the fifth wave of behaviorism: rewiring the stress response. EBT draws upon behavioral techniques, but targets the faulty stress wires that underpin what ails us (the first four waves) and the stress chemical cascade.

Oddly enough, these wires are easy to find because when we are stressed, what caused that stress is a wire – and that wire is being activated in real-time. Wires only change one way: by experience. The simple act of switching off that circuit does the trick. Not only do we experience immediate stress relief, but we update that wire. This is the ultimate two-in-one. How do we know that it's working? As the circuits change, we see spontaneous improvements in mood, thoughts, and behavior. We use the conscious mind and a few emotional techniques to change the unconscious mind. As it's the unconscious mind that fires automatically, we see changes in ourselves that surprise us.

For example, if you use cognitive methods to lose weight, you change your thoughts or environment to help you adhere to your food plan. With EBT, when you have a desire to overeat, you use the EBT tools to switch off the faulty wire. When the wire shuts off, your desire to overeat fades. You eat in a healthy way more naturally and with fewer cravings. The problem is the wire, not the behavior.

As you read this book, you might wonder why you have never heard about EBT and how it came about. I began developing EBT about 40 years ago, pregnant with my first child and on bed rest. As a faculty member in adolescent medicine and later, in family medicine at the University, I began searching for the root cause of obesity in children and adolescents. What was fueling the drive to overeat? I discovered research by Hilde Bruch, a Baylor College of Medicine psychiatrist, published in 1940, which suggested to me that that drive was being fueled by emotional disconnection.

In my youthful zeal, I quickly developed emotional techniques to promote connection. We taught them to families in the University clinic. Soon thereafter, the mother of a 10-year-old girl who was in this new "emotional connection" program approached me in the clinic. Her daughter had changed so radically that she wanted the tools for herself.

At the time, brain science was in its infancy, and I had no way to explain why her daughter was so happy, vibrant, and craving-free. However, I knew at that moment I would devote my career to finding out, and making the techniques available to people of all ages.

Since then, many scientists, clinicians, and health leaders have guided the development of EBT. In the early 2000s, a small group of us at UCSF brought the method to the next level of scientific rigor. We realized that we could use our emotional tools for rewiring the stress response in the emotional brain. As these circuits control our emotional and spiritual evolution as well as our health, EBT could become a new pathway to self-directed optimal well-being.

The method's development was packed with high drama, painful setbacks, and more than a few stalls. The two most dramatic moments occurred in late April 2007. First, Igor Mitrovic, a neuroscientist and physiologist, had the confidence and heart to turn away from the reductionist thinking common to scientists, which is to find esoteric pathways and small differences. Instead, he conceptualized all stress circuits as either effective ("stress-resilient") or ineffective ("stress-reactive"). This concept had a scientific backbone, corresponding to the homeostatic or allostatic physiological states. This was an essential breakthrough, giving us a way to name our circuits, categorize them, and then . . . crush, zap, and transform the ones that triggered toxic stress and blocked our joy. This enabled us to "get off the couch" and integrate rewiring circuits into our daily practice of living our best lives.

Second, in early iterations of the method, our global stress burden was decidedly lower. We could see impressive results with simple emotion-based techniques like asking,

"How do I feel?" and "What do I need?" That changed in the late 1990s and by 2007, I had a crisis of confidence in the previous iteration of the method. Stress levels were so high that we needed a new way for emotions to be regulated. This led me to rethink the emotional brain and the nature of emotions. Emotional processing was our genetically-imbued best way to release stress and take charge of our physiology. Emotions weren't just psychological, but the biological substrate of stress resilience and updating our automatic responses to daily life. They were processed differently based on our stress level. We identified five stress levels, each with a corresponding emotional technique. Both were consistent with attachment theory and neurophysiology. This became the EBT 5-Point System of Emotional and Behavioral Regulation.

In 2011, our EBT research team of Igor Mitrovic, Lynda Frassetto, Lindsey Fish, and I, proposed a new healthcare paradigm based on the method. Our article, "Rewiring the Stress Response: A New Paradigm in Healthcare," was published in a small medical journal. Then, in early 2013, we proposed a conceptual basis of the method as Emotional Plasticity Theory. Several researchers have studied the method's effectiveness, with ten studies conducted, all showing promising results.

One finding from University of Kentucky research on the method was that the use of the tools with others outside of the group sessions in "connections" by telephone was the best predictor of both health outcomes and how much participants liked the method. We set about building a technology platform to make it easier for people to connect with others to use the tools privately and remotely.

Last, as EBT targeted the same wires addressed by psychotherapy, we realized that most mental health professionals could find EBT useful. We began certifying psychologists and counselors in the method either to deliver it as a separate intervention or as a "bolt-on" to traditional therapy. Physicians began referring patients to EBT to add a physiological foundation to their medical treatments and perhaps improve health outcomes.

More research is needed. However, EBT has already crossed a hurdle that many other interventions have not. Currently, for treatments to be taken seriously, the first step is to propose a biological mechanism of action. We have proposed one – that EBT rewires the stress response.

The tools conform to what research has shown to be essential for rewiring stress. These stress circuits are core to survival so they are carefully protected and updated. Any way we respond when stressed, such as overeating, shaming ourselves, or feeling powerless or unworthy, is encoded in the emotional brain, then reactivated without our permission. This causes most of our "why do I keep on doing that?" moments.

To erase the circuit that causes that response, we must be in the same level of stress we were in when it was encoded, but to then do something differently. The circuit is updated and the old circuit is erased. This promotes lasting change. Cognitive methods (CBT, awareness, mindfulness, and others) do not stress-activate the wire, but instead provide new information to the circuit. That's helpful in the moment, but as it does not update the faulty wire, when stressful times come, that old circuit roars back and we do "what we keep on doing." This science offers one explanation for why our cognitive methods seem to work, but do not produce lasting results.

Also, when cognitive techniques were developed, research methods were not available to test whether or not they had the power to switch off the stress response. Recently, researchers at New York University tested cognitive methods and showed them to be lacking. Their research showed that even though people knew how to shut off stress when they were in low-stress states, in high stress those same techniques did not work. As cognitive methods are the mainstay of public health and psychotherapeutic approaches, this research sent a wave of alarm through the professional health community.

The EBT method is firmly grounded in science. Our outcome research to date is promising. It is consistent with changes one would expect if we were successful in addressing the root cause of most health-related problems – the emotional brain in stress overload. The tools are consistent with neurophysiology. Each brain stress level requires a different technique, as the brain's optimal emotional processing varies with the level of threat. The brain offers up a different resiliency pathway for a fight-or-flight dire need than it does for small upsets. To shape the tools for each brain state, we drew upon what highly-effective parents do to process their children's emotions at each stress level. Also, we learned from our participants, with now more than half a million people having used the method.

Since 2011, we have simplified and refined the method for rapid results and ease of use. We discovered that a mobile app made it easier to use the tools, especially in high-stress times, and that participants liked telegroups for their convenience and privacy. We learned to deliver small doses of EBT at the start and then add more tools over time.

When I began developing EBT, I was warned by members of the research community at the University that at some point the techniques must be "code-locked." We had to have a definitive program that could be studied over decades. In the last year, we accomplished that, with this book as an introduction, another on the 5-Point System, two 30-day programs for rewiring toxic stress circuits (stress overload and stress eating), and advanced 30-day courses, one on each of the seven rewards, for those who want to raise their brain's set point, the ultimate goal of EBT.

How do you start becoming comfortable with your emotional brain and using these techniques? You take it slowly and make it fun. The primitive, reptilian brain strongly prefers the old way of processing stress. Expect some resistance at first. For example, when computers were introduced at the University years ago to help us access cognitive content in a new way, I was a young faculty member. It was pretty unnerving at first. I remember thinking, "Can I opt out of this?" Then I experienced the life-changing benefits of the internet, and now, of course, I don't know what I would do without it. That same gradual appreciation of the EBT tools may occur for you.

My husband, Walt, suggested that this book focus on the one tool that, in his experience, delivers "80 percent of the benefits of EBT." His suggestion reminded me of something similar said by a medical student. It was during the last session of our EBT elective when each student shared the most important thing they had learned from the course. Most identified a neuroscience concept or a physiological mechanism. Then, the last student said, "The most important thing I learned from this course is that one simple tool can change your life."

This is the tool you will learn in this book. I hope you will enjoy discovering a new way to access the unique powers of your emotional brain, which are to give and receive love and to experience an abundance of the rewards that come from fulfilling your higher purpose.

I hope this stress solution – the ideas and this new technique – will change your life!

Part I.
The Pandemic of Toxic Stress

Chapter 1.
What's Happening?
It's Stress

Miranda was at her breaking point.

She said, "My sister is in the middle of a divorce. My husband, Todd, just broke his arm. I'm stuck at home. I'm bingeing on carbs, vodka, and Netflix. And now, the last straw . . . my company is downsizing due to Covid, and I'm in charge of letting people go. I'm ruining their lives! I'm awake half the night. What's happening to me?"

I said, "I'm sorry you're going through this. It's stress."

"This isn't just stress; it's worse than stress. It's toxic!"

"That's right, it's stress overload, which is why we all need something like a 'stress vaccine,' a scientific, easy-to-use way to release stress that has lasting effects."

I think of EBT as a stress vaccine because once Miranda learns the emotional techniques, she'll have them for life and, with each use, her neural pathways of resilience will become more dominant and more likely to fire spontaneously.

The method is so enlivening! It gives us the keys to the emotional brains' hidden pathways that take us from stress to joy. Using it can be disorienting! One moment, we are in stress, which is drab, miserable, and boring, and then, two to five minutes later, life is fascinating, bursting with possibility – and so much fun!

Miranda asked, "Is it therapy?"

"It's Emotional Brain Training, which is based on neuroplasticity. Each time you switch off stress, you change your wiring. Over time, your brain becomes wired for radical resilience, leaning into adversity and coming out the other side stronger, happier, and healthier."

Miranda said, "That sounds . . . magical!"

This method is a departure from traditional ways of coping. We're wiring in resilience, so we solve our problems and do not infect the world with our emotional clutter. In a way, this approach is much like environmental sustainability, except it is emotional sustainability. The parallels are stunning. The two most dangerous emissions of humans are the carbon dioxide that contributes to climate change and our stress-induced negative emotions that cause health and social problems. The accumulation of carbon makes our world unsafe, and the build-up of suppressed and harmfully-expressed emotions makes our world emotionally "hotter" and more treacherous. We need to draw down carbon dioxide levels, but also to draw down our levels of toxic emotions.

This is very easy to do, as it's not much of a financial reach. After reading this book, you will "own" a powerful technique for drawing down your emotional stress. However, accomplishing this as a nation is a pretty major educational reach. Yet the method is highly contagious.

When one person learns EBT, then other people become aware of it and they want to learn it, too. The purpose of this book is to provide an easy way to extend that educational reach.

What is this method? What is EBT?

It is a method of taking charge of what controls us – our emotional wiring. We have been taught to control our thoughts and behaviors, but what controls them are our neural circuits. We ARE our wires, they are the essence of our personal history and the drivers of our responses. The idea that we can control these wires – even to a small extent – is life-changing. If we want to change our thoughts, emotions, and behavior, we do that the brain-savvy way – we switch off the wires that spark them.

These circuits are so important because they color all aspects of our lives. The outside world – the images we see, the sounds we hear, and what we touch – comes into our brain, and depending upon which wire we activate, the world looks very different. We all have effective circuits that make even an overcast day seem bright and ineffective wires that make the day seem dark no matter what the weather.

To take charge of her emotional brain, Miranda will need to see stress through a new lens. Stress is toxic. It negatively and significantly impacts every cell in her body and every organ and organ system. As it only takes four minutes to switch off high-stress states, more often than not, when she feels stressed, she needs to "jump on it" and switch it off. This is an appealing concept because she can quickly experience four benefits:

First, she will notice how emotionally effective she is becoming. Her brain is becoming more "emotionally fluid" rather than being stuck in worry, irritability, depression, or numbness. Positive feelings flow – feeling grateful, happy, secure, and proud – and these emotions change her day.

Second, Miranda will feel more in control. If she is craving sugar or procrastinating about a work deadline, she has the personal pleasure of switching off those drives. This boosts her self-confidence as well as giving her a leg up in taking charge of her health and life.

Third, she will find far more joy in the natural pleasures of life. Stress wires drive us to use artificial rewards and addictive pleasures, while resilient wires activate neurotransmitter surges from natural pleasures. She may decide to take up painting, learn to tap dance, or plant a garden. Her passions will come alive!

Last, Miranda will build stress immunity. Each time she uses the technique, it adds to the cumulative effect based on Hebb's Law of neuroplasticity. Wires that fire together wire together and are more likely to fire together again. Her momentary choice to process her emotions causes her resilient wires to become stronger and weakens her reactive wires. Over time, this practice promotes raising her brain's set point or "stress habit" for lasting improvements in her health and well-being.

I said to Miranda, "Each time you are stressed and process your emotions, you switch off a reactive wire and activate a resilient wire. That resilient wire takes you to a state of supreme connection. The harmful stress chemicals stop surging and every cell of your being is steeped in healing chemicals. It's a brain reset. Every aspect of life looks and feels different – and far better."

"So if I am really irritated by Todd because he drank too much, fell down the stairs, and broke his arm, if I notice I'm stressed, and I use the technique, what happens?"

"You improve your emotional skills. You switch from feeling irritated and miserable to feeling pretty relaxed and reasonably happy."

"I want that."

"The process takes two steps. First, you talk about a situation that stresses you. Then you express strong, healthy anger. That clears the stress that would otherwise take your thinking brain offline. You pour out your emotions, and they flow from negative to positive. You will feel present and connected with a slight glow from your brain's reward center."

"I can do that part, all except anger. I don't like anger."

"I'll help you with that. The last step helps you take action and move forward with purpose. Would you like to try out the technique?"

Miranda hesitated, then replied, "I'm not sure."

"Wait until your emotional brain warms up to the idea."

"Okay, I'm warmed up. I'd like to try it."

I told her that the process is to say a few key words ("lead-ins") using her thinking brain ("prefrontal cortex") and then pause and wait for her emotional brain to respond. Her wires will be activated and soon thereafter, their hidden messages will appear in her mind as words. Once they appear in her mind, she will feel her feelings until they fade, and then go on to the next lead-in.

Her first step is to talk about what is bothering her by telling the story for about a minute.

Miranda said, "I don't know what to do about it . . ."

"You don't have to know. The words will appear in your brain. Your emotional brain will sort it out for you."

"The situation is . . . I am laying off employees. My sister is going through a really difficult divorce, my husband just had surgery, my stress is so high, and I am coping in very unhealthy ways."

"The next lead-in is: 'What I am most stressed about is . . .'"

"What I am most stressed about is . . . my sister. She is unhappy."

"Nicely done. Next see if you can express your emotions, first by expressing healthy anger. . . protest that your sister is unhappy."

"I feel angry that . . . she's unhappy. I can't stand it that . . . she's unhappy. I HATE it that . . . she is so unhappy! I hate that!"

"Now let your feelings flow in this order: sad, afraid, guilty, grateful, happy, secure, and proud."

"I feel sad that she is depressed . . . I feel afraid she will harm herself . . . I feel guilty that . . . I didn't follow my gut feeling ten years ago and tell her NOT to marry him . . . but I feel grateful that . . . she is starting a new life. I feel happy that . . . we are close. I feel secure that . . . this will pass . . . and I feel PROUD that . . . I am supporting her in her time of need."

Miranda had completed the first part of the method, enough to get an inkling of its power. She gasped and then asked, "What just happened? That was amazing!"

"You just changed your body chemistry. You shut off a wire that triggers the stress chemical cascade. You activated your brain's reward center and felt a surge of dopamine and endorphins."

"I feel *much* better! I feel a glow in my body!"

"Fantastic! Well done. Do you want to try the second step, which makes it easy to move forward with purpose?"

"Absolutely!"

"What do you expect of yourself?"

"I expect myself to do the best I can to . . . love and support my sister."

"Excellent. Say to yourself some encouraging words to help you follow through with your plan."

Miranda said, "I can do that!"

"You just created a challenging expectation. Now identify the essential pain, the hard part in following through, then feel your feelings until they fade."

"Hmmm . . . the essential pain is . . . it takes work, a lot of work."

"Feel that in your body, then turn your attention to the reason you will follow through, your higher purpose."

Miranda asked, "What are the choices?"

"Say whatever is true for you. To give you something to draw from, there are seven commonly used in EBT: sanctuary, authenticity, vibrancy, integrity, intimacy, spirituality, and freedom."

Miranda said, "All of them are important to me, but

the one that resonates the most with me is intimacy, giving and receiving love."

"What made you choose that one?"

"I want a healthy relationship with my sister. I love her. I want to give her love and feel her love."

"How do you feel now?"

She paused and then said, "I feel peaceful inside, and my body is glowing. That was magical."

Miranda had switched off the reactive wire that was the problem. It would become activated again before long, but even that one use of the technique mattered. It made a small but important improvement in her wiring – and she was becoming more comfortable with taking charge of her emotional brain.

Miranda asked, "So, EBT will help me change my brain's neural pathways?"

"That's right. The secret in using it is that these pathways are in the emotional brain, which is the seat of the soul and the motherboard of humanity. Using the tools has a ripple effect, changing you, and, as emotions are incredibly contagious, giving you a way to share your emotional wealth with others."

She said, "Tell me more . . ."

Chapter 2.

The Stress Brain

As a teenager, I had an "emotional eating problem" of sugar binges and my mother told me that I had an issue with "low self-esteem." I had no idea what to do about either of these things. Nor did I know that when a craving came on or I was feeling bad about myself, it was not an issue or problem. It was just a wire in my brain.

Knowing that one fact would have changed my life. I wouldn't have felt ashamed about my overeating or worried that I was psychologically broken. Instead, I would have shrugged and said, "Oh, I get it. That's one of those reactive wires." Then, I would have processed my emotions and the offending wire would have switched off. A resilient wire would then have guided my way, and for that moment at least, my suffering would have faded. Even more important, I would have known I was neither broken nor powerless, two lessons it would take me decades to learn.

With this new approach to self-care based on brain science, we can stop fretting about perceived issues and problems and focus on processing the emotions activated by those unwanted wires. Our thinking brain, or prefrontal cortex, does most of the work by using the technique. The wires it changes are stored in the emotional brain, the unconscious mind, which is comprised of the limbic brain and the reptilian brain. It's remarkably easy as the brain stores these wires in a highly organized way . . .

The 5 EBT Brain States

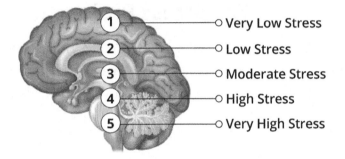

To keep it simple and practical, there are five different levels of stress in the brain in the EBT system. We number them from 1 to 5, and a different brain area is in charge at each stress level. Stress increases based on the level of real or perceived threat, and regardless of its veracity, the brain takes threats seriously, as its first priority other than procreation is survival. It puts the fastest, most extreme part of the brain in charge when it perceives that we are highly vulnerable, regardless of whether we are standing in a restaurant waiting for our blind date or being charged by a woolly mammoth.

It's normal to be in all five brain states on any given day, including going down to Brain State 4 where we feel bad or triggered, or to Brain State 5 in which we feel

Different Brain Areas Are in Charge

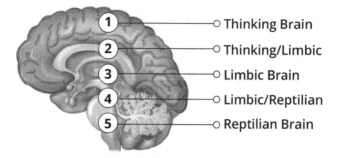

1 ───○ Thinking Brain
2 ───○ Thinking/Limbic
3 ───○ Limbic Brain
4 ───○ Limbic/Reptilian
5 ───○ Reptilian Brain

overwhelmed, lost, or addicted. In fact, after we have been in those states, assuming we know how to get out of them reasonably quickly, we may find ourselves more focused, innovative, or even transformed.

The key with these more stressed states is not to become stuck in them. Chronic stress is what harms us. When we are in Brain States 1 and 2, we are running resilient wires that are homeostatic. The term homeostasis was coined by physiologist Walter B. Cannon at the beginning of the 20th century. It is derived from the Greek words *homeo*, meaning "same," and *stasis*, meaning "stable," so "remaining stable by staying the same." Our homeostatic wires balance us out and keep us in the healthy zone in all aspects of physiology and domains of life.

Once we have outstripped the capacity of these protective homeostatic wires to take charge, we begin running reactive wires. We are in Brain States 3, 4, and 5, and the wires are allostatic. In 1988, neuroscientist Peter Sterling and biologist Joseph Eyer coined a new term, allostasis, derived from the Greek *allo*, which means "variable" and *stasis*. Allostasis is the process of regulating with behavioral or physiological changes that bust past homeostatic levels. These wires cause us to career out of control, departing from the physiologically healthy zone. They result in a build-up of stress ("allostatic load") that is currently our most accurate predictor of morbidity and mortality in humans.

We Can Be Resilient or Reactive

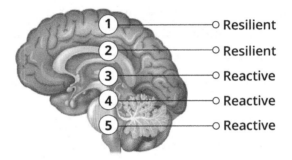

With these three concepts – stress levels, brain states, and wires – we now have a language that enables us to share what is happening in our most important body part, the emotional brain. Not being able to talk about what is really going on inside our body and brain keeps us from having clarity about how to feel better. If we know our brain state, we can do something about it. If we know that our reptilian brain is in charge of us at the moment, we can forgive ourselves for being a bit irritable or snappish. Last, if we know that what has triggered our state is a wire, then, given recent advances in neuroplasticity, we can set out with a plan to rewire it.

In the past, chatting about your emotional brain wasn't a common thing to do. People may talk about their heart ("getting my pulse down") or their abs ("working on my six-pack" or "getting rid of that belly fat"), but until now they probably didn't share how their limbic brain was doing or the state of their reptile within.

Most people know that the unconscious mind controls such things as our heart rate, our belly fat, and our chattiness, but not that it is in control of our brain state and set point. That is changing. You might even become one of the change agents when you mention your brain state to someone or refer to your wiring. For example, you might comment that you just triggered a reactive wire, and that it will rattle around for a while as those allostatic wires do. When checking out at the grocery store, when the clerk asks how you are doing, you might say, "I'm at Brain State 3 right now. How about you?"

Also, in your discussions with friends, they might speak in psychological terms, such as remarking that their spouse has abandonment issues or your co-worker has social anxiety problems. You might say, "That's so psychological. Issues and problems are all based on emotional brain wires. In fact, any thought, emotion, behavior, or response is the activation of a wire in the beautiful emotional brain."

The updated version of psychological talk is more along the lines of, "my spouse is running a reactive wire and he can't get out of Brain State 5. His reptilian brain is taking him for a ride." Or you might bring up your co-worker's social anxiety and say, "his circuits are so activated, if he expresses some healthy anger and switches off those neural pathways, he'll be just fine, even super secure and calm."

Sometimes this language creep happens slowly, but sharing brain states and wires is so helpful that it has been catching on. Many couples, families, and organizations have adopted it in the last few years. In a recent staff meeting at EBT, one team member was challenging to communicate with. After the meeting, another staff member said, "I didn't think anything of it. He was at Brain State 5. It will pass."

Integrating these concepts about stress levels, brain states, and wires gives us a new way to understand that we have a body and brain that seem stable, but given the range of states and the options for wires we can run, our inner lives are inherently unstable. Our brain state varies, and that is consistent with the survival of the species. When we're running up a grassy hill, our heart rate is fast, and when we are curled up on the couch with a good book, our heart rate is slow. Brain states are variable like that.

Our Brain State Impacts Us

Brain State	Thoughts	Feelings	Relationships	Behavior	Health
1	Abstract	Joyous	Intimate	Optimal	Excellent
2	Concrete	Balanced	Companionable	Healthy	Good
3	Rigid	Mixed	Social	Moderate	Fair
4	Reactive	Unbalanced	Detached/Needy	Unhealthy	Poor
5	Irrational	Overwhelmed	Disengaged/Merged	Destructive	Very Poor

What's been missing is a way to integrate our neurophysiology with our functioning. On the table above are characteristics based on brain states. Our thoughts, feelings, relationships, behavior, and health can vary widely.

If you don't know that when you're at Brain State 5 it is perfectly normal to be irrational, overwhelmed, disengaged or merged in relationships, with destructive habits and very poor health, you might judge yourself. What the emotional brain can't stand is self-judgment, so just knowing that we have five people inside us based on brain state and that is normal can help stop the self-judgment that prolongs and exacerbates toxic stress.

In sharing these ideas with Miranda, it was the brain state characteristics that moved her the most.

Miranda said, "When I'm at 5, I am so hard on myself. I've always assumed that the problem was me, that I must be a little crazy."

I said, "Everyone is extreme at Brain State 5, especially when we become stuck there, but the cause is stress, and who isn't stressed these days?"

She said, "Nobody."

"With the Covid crisis, we were caught by surprise, and then most of the rules of life we thought were enduring changed. Everyone went to Brain State 5."

"Everyone in my family was at 4 or 5, and yet we experienced it so differently."

"Everyone is about the same at Brain State 1 – kind, loving, bright, and aware – but the more the brain goes into stress, the more extreme and diverse our characteristics. What's more, each extreme domain of life makes it harder to treat the other domains. The problem is the brain state, not any one characteristic."

"Todd was forgetful, depressed, and distant. He was drinking too much and that is why he tripped on the stairs and broke his arm. I became so anxious that I started bingeing on carbs, vodka, and Netflix, and losing myself in Todd's issues and my sister's problems."

"Miranda, the Covid crisis will pass, but if you use this time to reset your approach to life based on the science of the emotional brain, you'll have more compassion for yourself and others, and be happier and healthier."

Other than the risks from impulsive behaviors and accidents, short-term stress is not the problem. It is when those reactive wires begin to be dominant, driving down our brain's conditioned stress level ("set point") so it is in the allostatic range, that more problems arise. This is why the ultimate goal of EBT is to raise the brain's set point. Then we can still be in all five states in any day, but with the brain's default state in homeostasis, preferably Brain State 1.

We can control our wiring, but doing so involves understanding our emotions and tapping into their astonishing power.

Chapter 3.

Emotions and Stress

Two years ago, when people were still gathering in crowds, I attended Paul Simon's farewell concert at the Oakland Coliseum. The place was packed, and late in the evening, Paul opened up to questions. One fan asked him how he wrote his songs.

Paul paused, then looked upward, as if to the heavens. With a huge sweep of his arms extending all the way around his body, he said, "They flow through me."

It was as if some force invaded his body, flowed through his being, and out the other side came this extraordinary creation of music and lyrics.

Whoosh!

I realized that is just what happens when we use emotions to glide along the emotional brain's resiliency pathways. Think of it this way: The stress of the world enters our brain and our emotions get stuck. That will always be the case, but if we trust the nature of life and appreciate that we can process our stuck emotions and allow healing, fluid feelings to flow through us, that changes our life.

When I shared this with Miranda, she understood instantly.

She said, "That's what happens for me. The stress enters my brain, and I get blocked. I need to flow through it."

Miranda continued, "I don't express my feelings. Instead, I get very busy or quit work for the day and cope in unhealthy ways."

"What stands between you and feeling fantastic is unpacking your emotions and getting them to flow."

"I immediately try to fix it. I make lists, blame myself, or exhaust myself and give up."

"It's not your fault, Miranda! Who told you that the problem was blocked emotions and that you could make them flow?"

"Nobody. I thought the problem was me."

We are all Miranda. Nobody comes into adulthood without some reactive wires. I was never taught that when I felt disconnected, the problem was not me but that my emotions weren't flowing. When people talk about their abandonment issues, their triggered addictions, and the way they have a fundamental sense that they do not exist, they are not worthy, or that something is broken in them, they have not yet become comfortable with their emotional brain.

They do not know that, like all of us, they have a few reactive wires that were encoded through no fault of their own and without their permission. The emotional brain takes all comers and then has the audacity to store our reactive wires at the bottom of the brain in its least plastic area.

We are always just one or two doses of the technique away from turning emotional blocks into emotional flows.

This is our biological asset. Our genes make us astonishingly powerful, but there is only one caveat: we must surrender. We must accept that stress from our past experiences is stored in our brain and reactivated in response to current situations – and to switch off that stress, we must feel.

When stress arrives in our brain, a reactive wire is triggered, and we are always at a crossroads. The choice is either to stay present to our feelings, ugly though they might be, and process them, or not. If we stay the course and process our emotions, the reactive wire switches off, and a resilient wire takes us up and over to our joy. We can't even remember how bad we felt. In fact, we feel that glow of pride that we stayed the emotional course.

I said to Miranda, "Do you realize how strong you are? You have an emotional brain with pathways that will quiet your mind, soothe your soul, and help you take purposeful actions. However, you cannot get on those resiliency pathways unless you are willing to connect with yourself and rifle through your gritty negative emotions for a few moments. Then the drama is over, and you are in connection, purpose, and joy."

She said, "I fear that if I ever started to feel my feelings, I'd go so low for so long that I would never recover."

"That may have been true in the past, but now you have EBT."

"I'm tired! I'm SCARED! This takes too much work!"

"I understand, but do you appreciate how much work it is to *not* process your feelings? That is much harder!"

If we choose not to process our strong emotions, the reactive wires win. None of them are pretty, and all of them cause us suffering. There are two kinds of reactive wires.

One type of reactive wire is a survival circuit. For example, in some random stressful situations, when we're in fight-or-flight mode, we do whatever it takes to feel better – eat, drink, go numb, text, procrastinate, or countless other possibilities. The brain encodes these survival circuits to help us out. Whatever we feel, do, or think in order to feel better when we are stressed, the brain encodes that false association into a reactive circuit. Then it replays that wire even in response to normal daily stress.

I said to Miranda, "Do you have any reactive neural pathways that cause you to repeat old patterns even though you promise yourself that you will not?"

She said, "Are you kidding? I have dozens of them. I have a perfectionist circuit, a control-freak wire, an I-want-to-drink-vodka pathway, and a crazy-for-carbs circuit, too. The worst one is my constant worrying."

"What I'm telling you is that when one of those wires is activated, you can't think your way out of it."

"I know that, but why?"

"An emotional wall within blocks you, such as worrying, going numb, feeling irritable, or being depressed. You can learn how to notice that emotional wall and not judge it, as the emotional brain can't stand judgments. It's about love. Once you do that, you move forward and tear down that wall. It's just skill and you can learn it."

"That's motivating to me."

"Wonderful! We all have these survival circuits, but we also have another, deeper kind of wire that we can use the same techniques to unblock, too. Then our emotions flow through us, and we get unstuck."

The other type of reactive circuit in the emotional brain is a core circuit. The survival circuits cause triggering, but these core circuits are even more unsettling. They are ridiculous core beliefs. The brain encodes these false generalizations during stressful moments, often early in life, when the brain strongly remembers adverse experiences, or later in adulthood when changes, losses, or upsets overwhelmed our capacity to process our emotions.

In that moment of overwhelm, we really did experience not existing, having no power, or sensing that we were bad. The feeling was momentary, but the brain encoded a neural pathway that tells us it always has been true, it is true now, and it will always be true.

I said, "When the brain happens to activate these wires, we feel like we are back to being six years old or whatever age we were when we had that experience."

These activations typically occur quite often or even become chronic. Even though they were encoded during childhood or later when we were completely stressed out, the brain does not put them in context. For example, one of my core circuits was, "I am not worthy." When I was running a resilient wire, I felt worthy, and could not imagine feeling unworthy, inadequate, or less than. But all it took was some small stressful situation, and my reactive wire would be triggered, and a momentary early experience when I felt unworthy filled me with shame. Instead of my brain telling me: "Once when you were at school and that girl Jan was bullying you, you thought you were unworthy," it told me: "You are unworthy. You always have been unworthy. You always will be unworthy."

Stress Decreases Self-Control

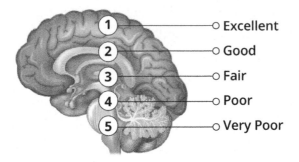

Life is difficult enough without having errant wires with ridiculous messages being activated throughout the day. The choice is clear. One option is that we live with these wires and try to work around them, which usually involves serious losses, such as taking more medications, avoiding people who trigger us, or, the most common, suffering in silence.

The other option is that we take the vulnerable but brave approach and process our emotions. We switch off the activated wire. All the resilient wires that take over when the reactive wire has been dismissed lead to Brain State 1, as optimal physiology is the goal of self-regulation. That's a natural process that we tap into by using the techniques of EBT.

Our mindset changes radically. All those reactive wires – the triggered survival circuits and the faulty core beliefs – are gone, and encouraging, healthy, and positive wires take over. It's quite startling to spiral up to One and, at first, almost creepy. The reality that we are our wires and that we can "play" with them, switching them off and on, is tremendously exciting. However, there is resistance from the reptilian brain as it prefers the status quo. It takes repeated experience in using the technique to win over the lizard brain and to become comfortable with feeling as great as we can feel.

Stress Makes Emotions Toxic

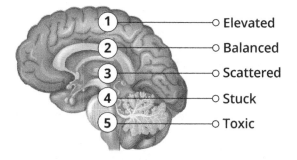

1 —o Elevated
2 —o Balanced
3 —o Scattered
4 —o Stuck
5 —o Toxic

In reality, the scattered, stuck, and toxic emotions are all amalgams of unexpressed anger, sadness, fear, and guilt that EBT enables us to tease apart, detoxify, and clear. However, to become comfortable with your emotional brain, let's take a closer look at each of the five brain states.

Brain State 1
Executive Control: Excellent
Emotions: Elevated

When we are at Brain State 1, our executive control is excellent, and our emotions are elevated, such as love, compassion, gratitude, hope, forgiveness, awe, and joy. Our emotions do not tell us what we need because we have no needs other than to experience them. Our basic needs for safety, love, comfort, and pleasure have been met, and, at least for a moment, we can feel the glow.

In a supremely integrated state, both brain hemispheres, plus our thinking and emotional brains, as well as our brain and our body, are all connected. Our entire physiology is at its best, and our prefrontal cortex is so highly functional that we can focus our attention on our elevated emotions and savor them.

A limiting factor in life is our "self-regulatory strength," or our capacity to stay connected to our emotions and manage our lives. At One, we have such an abundance of that strength that we can not only stay present and aware but also think of our higher purpose for what we are doing. The thought of that higher purpose activates rewards and blocks the hypothalamus ("stress trigger") from being activated.

I asked Miranda, "When you have cleared away stress, what positive emotion are you apt to feel?"

She said, "The only one I can think of now is love. I felt a surge of loving feelings for Todd this morning when I woke up."

"Can you describe those feelings?"

"Not really. Words aren't enough."

As much as Brain State 1's emotions are ethereal and sublime, the most important point about this state is that it gives us a profound capacity to give back and be of service. All our needs are met, and the whole range of artificial pleasures that have a high addiction potential do not interest us. This connected state gives us a protective shield against stress, and we are grounded in reality. These elevated emotions go beyond happiness, which can be separated from reality. All elevated emotions encapsulate the realities of life. For example, when we see a loved one and swoon, part of us feels the pain that soon there will be a parting. This essential pain amplifies the positive emotion and signals us that life is precious – and to make the most of it.

Brain State 2
Executive Control: Good
Emotions: Balanced

At Brain State 2, executive control is good, and feelings are balanced. This is a functional, transactional state in which the feelings that arise tell us what we really need. The emotional brain is our threat detector and searches for the whole range of possible threats – psychological, physical, or metabolic. It identifies our most important need, then "bubbles up" a feeling to the conscious mind that guides us to meet that need.

I asked Miranda, "Can you think of a time when you were at Brain State 2, low stress?"

She said, "This morning. It was a good morning. I was cooking breakfast, Todd and I were chatting, and it was pretty nice."

"How did you make decisions about whether you were going to chat with Todd, focus on cooking, or call your sister?"

"It happened naturally, I guess."

At Brain State 2, we have feelings that accurately tell us what we need. Most responses in life are automatic, as our emotions do most of the decision-making work for us. We can listen to our feelings, and they usher us forward to meet our most important needs.

When stress mounts and the homeostatic emotions depart, the allostatic emotions take over. Not only is the executive functioning that we rely on for being aware of our feelings and taking care of our needs faltering, but the emotions we feel are untrustworthy. They do not direct us to meet our needs. What do we need when we are at Brain States 3, 4, and 5? We only need one thing: a return to a homeostatic state, Brain State 2, or preferably, Brain State 1. Our executive control then becomes good or excellent, our emotions balanced or elevated, and those issues and problems fueled by reactive wires shut off.

Brain State 3
Executive Control: Fair
Emotions: Scattered

Brain State 3 is the most crucial stress level. It's our first step into allostasis, and yet we still have enough neocortical functioning to switch off reactive mode and activate a beautiful resiliency that brings us to Brain State 1.

In the days when we thought of stress as just tension, rather than the deleterious transformation of our entire physiology, we could write off Brain State 3. What's particularly significant about this "a little stressed" state is that the reactive wires often co-activate, and once we slip into Brain State 3, we run the risk of transitioning into Brain State 4 or 5.

As you take doses of EBT, you'll probably develop a personal policy about when to use it. If you're only a little stressed, you might decide to let it go, but if we don't take our stress seriously, once we're in allostasis, things tend to go downhill. The emotional brain is happy to shuttle us onto our resiliency pathways, but if we drift down to a stressed state and do not do anything about it, often it delivers more extreme consequences: a more stuck and toxic state of stress. All this is in service of the evolutionary goal of pointing our attention toward the best state for the survival of the species: One.

When I was raising my children, I traveled to give talks in short bursts, then arrived home, got them off to school, and settled down to write. Often, I was at Brain State 3, tired but ready to catch up on some work. I told myself that I didn't need to get to One, as after racing to catch planes and cramming myself into narrow airline seats, being at 3 was pretty good!

The chemical reality is that there are no safe brain states when we are running reactive wires. Allostasis is like that, and given that there is a major negative bias in the brain toward overestimating threats, any errant fearful thought I might have could spiral me down to a 4 or 5 – and the lizard brain would own me for a time.

Before long, my fingers would be dancing over the keys and I would be completely amazed at how prolific I was, thinking, "I have never written better! Maybe I didn't need that remedial course in Strunk and White's grammar book after all!" I was on a false high psychologically, but meanwhile, my brain state had slipped into the 4-to-5 range. Hours later, when I looked in horror at what I had written, I would invariably press the delete key. Since then, I have updated my policy: If I'm not at One, I take a break. Get to One, and don't settle for a Brain State 3. We don't have to settle anymore, as it only takes four minutes or less to get to One.

What's actually happening in Brain State 3? The connection between our prefrontal cortex and the emotional brain is iffy at best. We have lots of diverse feelings, but none is dominant. It's so confusing and so anxiety-provoking, as we do not stay long enough with one feeling to identify what we need.

Perhaps the most challenging aspect of Brain State 3 is that it is demanding. It does not feel good, and this stress is unnecessary. We can feel so much better rather quickly. Also, it's unproductive. We put the effort in, but wonder if we are really accomplishing anything. Even one state above this – Brain State 2 – and we can be so focused and productive that we amaze ourselves. Even one brain state up makes a huge difference!

Miranda said, "At Brain State 3, I don't have any one feeling. I start overthinking or I get anxious."

"Then what do you do?"

"I start worrying because I don't know what to do. I second-guess myself, and my 'I have to be perfect wire' shows up. I start thinking about all the mistakes I have made, and I lose confidence in myself. My sense of humor vanishes."

"What about relationships?"

"They are not bad, but I don't feel authentic. I have a harder time knowing who I am, so I can chat with people and look like I'm listening, but my mind is elsewhere."

"Then what happens?"

"Not much."

Emotions at Brain State 3 are scattered, and they can drift into the stuck or toxic category pretty easily. However, the worst part of Brain State 3 is that we do not feel securely connected to the deepest part of ourselves. We can neither give nor receive love, as the brain is very picky when it comes to love, as a way of delivering intimacy only if we bite the bullet, crash through these confusing, diverse emotions, and return to that connected state.

Miranda concluded, "Scattered describes it. Thinking too much, anxious, and tense."

Brain State 4
Executive Control: Poor
Emotions: Stuck

At Brain State 4, stress arousal levels increase. This is bad news for the brain's executive functioning, as stress biases the brain to focus narrowly on the current stressor. Whatever stresses us seems like *the only thing* that really matters, causing reactivity, obsessiveness, and compulsivity. We block out all the positive stimuli and easily become overwhelmed. Our emotions are ineffective – they do not tell us what we need – and extreme – we may feel no emotions or impossibly strong ones.

Brain State 4 can crop up anytime, often when we least expect it. Last night, I was happily walking around the house, as I just had hip surgery and I could actually walk! The dog was next to me and she jumped toward me, and I tripped over her, stumbling onto the floor. Instantly, I was at Brain State 4. I was in an altered state! Had I harmed my hip? Was the dog okay? And of course, how could I be so careless as to trip over the dog?

My emotions, which had been balanced, were now stuck. I was not angry, but hostile, at myself, at my hip, and at life. Granted, Brain State 4 is not very logical. Moments before, when I was at Brain State 2, I could trust my emotions. Not now! The emotions that flowed when I was in Brain State 2, now that I was in a higher stress state, became stuck. The sweet flowing emotions were now stalled. I was anxious, ashamed, numb, and overwhelmed. I didn't know what I needed, in fact, I couldn't even think!

The most important thing to remember about Brain State 4's emotions is that they do not tell you what you need. To know what you need takes doing something revolutionary – spiraling up to One. However, knowing that you are at Brain State 4 is rather tricky as there are three "emotional stress styles" and two of the three are stealthy. Most people do not know that they are stressed states.

The first is an unnecessary low, such as depression, anxiety, panic, or shame. It's easy to know if that's your emotional stress style because it feels bad and, at the very least, the discomfort of those states can get your attention.

The second emotional stress style is to have no feelings. Think of a deer in the headlights. Many people who have this style believe they have no stress. Perhaps they ease stress with eating, drinking, spending, working, or other options, but overall, they have no feelings.

The last of the three emotional stress styles is a false high. This is the most challenging style of stuck emotions because it feels so good! What's more, it's difficult to distinguish from a natural high, so we might think we are at One, and, based on our physiology, be at Brain State 4. We have the illusion that everything is fantastic, and only later when we awake from that state (often much later), do we realize we are hurting ourselves or others.

My emotional stress style is an unnecessary low, typically anxiety or depression, however, there are times when I am on a false high. Check which of the three apply to you to help you know when you're at Brain State 4 and emotions are stuck. Both core circuits and survival circuits are launched with a quick, subcortical emotional activation that unleashes strong drives for maladaptive behaviors or unreasonable beliefs that stress us out. Often both are triggered and we feel disconnected and have strong drives to find something that makes us feel safe, comforted, loved, or pleasured. This is what happened for Miranda.

She said, "Last night I was at Brain State 4, running a reactive wire, and I knew for sure that I needed banana bread. Was I hungry? Probably not, but I didn't care. I wanted something sweet. I was anxious after watching the news."

"What did you do?"

"I ate one slice of banana bread, but it wasn't enough. Then I had a second slice. Next, I really wanted some ice cream. I cut a third slice of banana bread, added a very large scoop of French vanilla ice cream, and then ate that."

"How did the rest of your evening go?"

"I didn't do anything, except I went online and bought some books and some environmentally-sensitive recycled plastic shoes for myself and then I watched videos."

Miranda's emotions were stuck, first anxiety, then a false high, and she had no idea what she really needed, which was to take a dose of EBT and spiral up to One, where her sensibility would magically reappear.

Brain State 5
Executive Control: Very Poor
Emotions: Toxic

At Brain State 5, executive control is offline, and feelings are toxic. This is a completely dysfunctional state, and we either dissociate and become numb, or we hyperarouse with exceedingly strong emotions. We do not know what we need and feel lost, confused, or overwhelmed.

The messages from the reactive wires are so strong and extreme that they "own" us. Although we can be at Brain State 5 because of situational stress, the most common cause of Brain State 5 is an errant neural pathway encoded during a traumatic experience. Any random sensation, emotion, thought, behavior, or state can trigger these strong reactive wires and bring us right back to a traumatic incident. This is the brain's effort to give us an opportunity to stay present to our toxic emotions and, if we do, begin to heal that hurt. However, often our brain shuts off so that we lose that opportunity to heal and stop living in the past.

What we need when we are at Brain State 5 and under the influence of toxic emotions is to process them and get to Brain State 1 again. Often that takes not only using the emotional tools and connecting to the deepest part of ourselves but being with someone who will listen to us with empathy as we process our emotions. Another person's rapt attention makes it easier for the thinking brain to be functional enough to feel our intense negative feelings so that they will transform into elevated emotions.

That is the power of human connection.

I said, "Miranda, when we're at Brain State 5, we need emotional connection. When we experience even a small amount of it, often it can take us to One."

Miranda said, "That happened for me when Todd came home from the hospital after he broke his arm. At first, I was so angry at him because his drinking caused his accident, and then I saw the expression on his face. He felt really ashamed of what he had done. Then he reached over to me and said, 'Miranda, I love you,' and he placed his hand on mine. I don't know whether it was his touch, his voice, his words, my relief, my compassion for him, or the light in the room, but I felt so much love for him. I stopped being mad. Nothing else mattered at that moment."

Where do these multilayered magical experiences come from? They are a special gift of the emotional brain in connection. What we do not realize is that each and every moment when our emotions are blocked, and we feel abandoned, depressed, terrified, or numb, we are within reach of Brain State 1.

We do not have to analyze what is wrong with us, make lists of what we will do, or blame ourselves for not being perfect. Instead, all we need is to appreciate that our thinking brain is disconnected from our emotional brain so we are cut off from the source of our personal power. Our emotions are blocked.

The solution is to use our emotions so that they flow, and we can transition from any stressed-out state back to Brain State 1. The solution is to trust our inherent strength, goodness, and wisdom – and to spiral up.

Chapter 4.

The Virus: Toxic Stress

The coronavirus pandemic has been wearing away at our bodies and brains. At first, people were scared, then anxiety set in, then depression, and more recently, numbness. The stress load ("allostatic load") on the brain and body is cumulative.

The more episodes of stress overload, the more reactive wires become stronger and more dominant. They grow. Emotions stop flowing through us and become stuck or toxic, but there is something we can do about it. We can focus on using each moment of stress to break up one of those reactive wires – the stress virus – and turn it into a resilient wire – an antibody.

This ongoing project of building stress antibodies to create radical resilience becomes our most powerful way to improve our lives, especially during these challenging times. It doesn't matter what we are stressed about. By taking a dose of EBT, we are enhancing our brain's emotional architecture and our capacity to find peace and power from within.

David was stressed about work and love.

He said, "I am closing my restaurant chain due to Covid. I feel like a deer in the headlights, I can't think, I am in panic mode, and my new girlfriend Lana just informed me that she is lonely. I'm not emotionally available enough for her. Laurel, I need a dose, a really big one."

David explained that Lana was the first woman with whom he felt deeply connected and excited, as if he were coming home. Yet he was also dismantling his business and felt pulled in all directions trying to balance love and work.

"I'm sorry you're going through this. You did the right thing to call for a coaching appointment because the more stressed you are, the more processing your emotions will be highly effective. Taking a dose will dismantle wires of reactivity and create wires of resilience. Let's make the most of that opportunity."

"That's what I want to do . . ."

"Wonderful. Whenever you are ready to begin . . ."

"The situation is . . . I think I love Lana. I am in a crisis with my work. My partners are nowhere to be found. I have to make all the decisions. There are boxes and furniture everywhere. And it is all falling on me. Then last night, Lana told me that she is lonely and that I am emotionally unavailable. Instead of supporting me, she's adding to my stress."

"What I am most stressed about is . . ."

"What I am most stressed about is . . . she is so needy and demanding!"

"Pause, you have activated the wire. Can you feel that in your body?"

The Reactive Wire

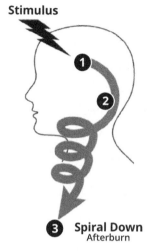

Stimulus

① Inaccurate Emotions
A stimulus enters the brain and causes overreactions (e.g., anxiety, numbness, panic). We do not know what we need.

② Unreasonable Expectations
Unconscious, ineffective beliefs take charge, increasing our stress. (e.g., I am not worthy, I have no power)

③ Ineffective Response
We take action in ways that do not meet our needs and cause us to spiral down into toxic stress overload.

③ Spiral Down
Afterburn

"In my throat, in my chest, I'm right on the edge . . ."

Just by talking about what was bothering him, David was starting to turn around his inner life. The formidable reactive circuit that had been ruling him, particularly since Lana told him she was lonely and said he was emotionally absent, was sending him into stress overload.

When that happens to you, see if you can bring up an image of a wire, a really gnarly one. The problem is not you. It's the wire that your brain activated to respond to your life's circumstances in that moment.

You may be able to identify the moment it was triggered, as the first part of a circuit's activation is an emotional response. As you experience emotions in your body, you can trust your body to tell you when you've been triggered. What you're looking for is an emotional response that makes no sense. It is either an overreaction or an underreaction. If something really bad happens, and instantly, you have no feelings, that's an underreaction. If a lesser problem crops up and your body signals that you are terrified, probably not going to survive this, it's an overreaction. Both are signs of the first phase of an activation of a reactive wire. In David's situation, his circuit caused him to overreact and feel as if he were going to be obliterated. This response was not a "psychological issue" but a biological response. A cascade of stress hormones was driving it.

The second phase of triggering a reactive wire is to launch ineffective expectations. The circuit tells you to do something about the threat and activates a drive to do it. This is unconscious at first, then becomes conscious, and you might think you could then use smart thinking and draw wisely upon your experiences to decide if you are going to do what your circuit tells you to do. Unfortunately, when a reactive wire is triggered, the prefrontal cortex does not function well, and the reactive circuit is already busy activating other reactive wires.

This is the drama! The ineffective expectations may be telling you to do things that make the problem worse, or they could be pummeling you with very damaging beliefs, or both. For our hunter-gatherer ancestors to have survived, they had to believe those instructions, so any and all of the unreasonable expectations ring absolutely true to us. There is no question about it! We know for sure that we absolutely must do what the circuit says, and those ineffective beliefs, such as that we are bad, have no power, or are not worthy? They seem true, too.

The last phase of a reactive wire activation is the response itself. By that time, we are being controlled by the wire, and whatever that response is, it is not effective. These wires make us repeat the same patterns, such as overeating, overspending, criticizing, people-pleasing, and other unhealthy, compulsive, and addictive responses. You might find yourself responding and later on asking, "Why did I do that?" but at the time, you are so toxified by stress that this response seems smart and wise, and no other response even comes under consideration. This one thing is the right thing to do! That's how powerful these reactive wires can be.

David had learned enough about EBT that at the time of his conversation with Lana, he had felt the urge to lash out at her, and even though every cell of his body wanted to, she was important enough to him, and the circuit was weak enough, that he had minimized the harm by not lashing out. He had reassured her that he cared about her, but inside, the circuit was buzzing. As these wires have no internal shut-off valves, he had a few drinks, watched some television, and, completely exhausted and rather numb, drifted off to sleep.

Now, in our session, he was talking about the stressful situation. By bringing it to mind, David activated the reactive circuits that impacted him during his conversation with Lana. That simple act of talking about it, as well as expressing a quick burst of healthy anger, had multiple beneficial effects: bringing up the unwanted wire, unlocking the synaptic connections between its neurons, and readying them to be updated and then locked away in a new and improved form in his unconscious mind. This is phenomenal! Our emotional brain does this automatically, giving us the option to transform whatever circuit dares to trigger us!

This astonishing capacity of the brain – that we can purposefully activate an annoying or undesirable response – has significant implications for how we take care of our emotional health. Although David's conflict with Lana seemed to be a real-time relationship issue, it was really an opportunity to update an outdated or ineffective wire that was encoded during childhood, when the brain strongly remembers our experiences, or later, during challenging times. Psychotherapy is designed to help us rewire these circuits, but David was now learning how to give himself doses of the stress vaccine as his self-care approach to emotional health. Once he learned it, he could use it alone, or for added effectiveness, with a peer, a small peer group, or his psychotherapist. This skill is versatile.

David had begun to grasp the deeper impacts of learning these skills and I could feel his energy shifting. Hope was in the air. With this technique, he could bring to mind a complex interchange with Lana, activate the wire that had triggered him, and then release its pent-up stress. Then he could transform it into a wire that gave him clarity and resilience. How uplifting! The pandemic had exhausted him and whittled away his sense of personal power. Now, he had it back as he could control his wires!

That emotional boost David felt is at the heart of EBT, as the tools are designed to empower us to take charge of our lives. The conceptual basis of the method is so simple. If you are in stress for whatever reason, process your emotions to switch off the offending wire and activate a new and better one. In this new wave of behaviorism, the wires are the target, not a thought, emotion, or behavior.

The timing is right for this method because the science has shown us that the first four waves of behaviorism, which relied on cognitive processing (CBT, mindfulness, acceptance), may not be sufficiently effective for our high-stress life today. In 2013, Candace Raio and colleagues' research at New York University showed that cognitive processing switched off stress activations in low-stress conditions. However, in higher-stress conditions that mirrored the stress level of pre-Covid times, it "failed the stress test."

Now stress levels are far higher than when this study was performed, so we sorely need a new, science-based strategy to prevail over toxic stress. The science of emotional plasticity theory upon which EBT is based offers a new option. In this theory, all creatures have survival drives (reactive wires that are extreme and send us to Brain State 5), which are brought forward in time by encoding circuits. Our efforts focus on taking charge of those circuits. What's most pernicious about survival circuits is that, based on associative learning, they can wire together with other circuits, giving them new power to control our responses.

Here's how it works: when a fight-or-flight wire and any random thought, emotion, or behavior are activated at the same time ("coactivating"), a new survival circuit is encoded. Then, with subsequent firings, the drive to repeat that previously-tame pattern transforms into a response that has fight-or-flight intensity. This is negative emotional plasticity. For example, yearn for an unavailable parent's love early in life, and the resultant survival circuit drives us to seek out unavailable partners as an adult and to find more-emotionally-available suitors undesirable. Or, turn to food for comfort when life seems to be falling apart, and a survival drive to overeat can follow. We can't get enough food because it's not body hunger that we are trying to satisfy. The problem is not psychological but biological: it's an errant survival circuit. Not only is this rogue wire exceedingly powerful but the brain blocks us from rewiring it unless certain conditions are met: attain the same level of stress again and stay present to the strong emotions it unleashes. The same emotional skill insufficiency that made us vulnerable to the encoding of the wire now could keep us from clearing it.

Most of our intractable and refractory problems, ranging from love addiction and opioid overdoses to compulsive texting and social anxiety, are fueled by survival circuits. The brain encodes these circuits in a flash without our permission or awareness, so it's no wonder that we can develop reflexive, addictive drives for almost anything! With unprecedented levels of stress pouring into our brains, now survival circuits are being encoded in our brains at an appalling rate. The extremes of the world take up residence inside us.

Yet this is only part of the story. When we're stressed for any reason, the thinking brain unleashes a cavalcade of ineffective thoughts, feelings, and behaviors that also activate reactive wires. These two experiences can be blended as reactive circuits trigger other reactive circuits in daily life's ongoing emotional journey. Scientists have differentiated the fight-or-flight response's survival drives and those activated by thoughts and feelings emanating from the neocortex.

NYU's Joseph LeDoux distinguished the survival drive "emotions" activated by the fight-or-flight response, from conscious experiences, or "feelings," that arise from the neocortex. Claire Weekes, an innovator in emotional health, similarly described a two-step system. According to Weekes, the first step is the activation of the "nervous" system, and the second step is the distorted thoughts of the neocortex that amplify stress. She believed that people with anxiety put the brakes on their feelings after the first activation and became emotion-avoidant, missing the opportunity to mitigate stress overload damage. She proposed the existence of an underlying problem: the fear of fear itself.

Despite advances in how we think about the stress response, toxic stress – messy though it is – remains pretty simple. It's the activation of a reactive wire, something that impacts all of us. The contribution of EBT is to keep it simple; use tools that shut off the reactive wires, regardless of the system that initially activated them. The method also gives us insight into why it has been so hard to develop the habit of processing strong emotions when stress overload comes our way.

First, some extremely reactive circuits can cause a "deer-in-the-headlights" response, in which our brain won't allow us to feel. It's not that we *don't feel*, but that we dissociate and the brain *won't let us feel*.

Second, with cognitive approaches showing limited effectiveness in deactivating strong negative emotions, who wants to tangle with those toxic emotions? Try to stop an eating binge halfway through consuming a pint of ice cream or untangle yourself from a heated quarrel right when you are about to make a good point, and all the positive thinking in the world will not switch off these drives.

Third, when we come up against a brick wall of toxic feelings, the brain cooperates and encodes an alternate neural pathway to reduce threat and access rewards. It becomes a survival circuit in its own right, whether it's a reflexive drive for numbness, rage, anxiety, or depression, or a behavioral option, like eating, drinking, spending, or texting.

Last, as chronic stress becomes our habit, the brain adjusts and favors an allostatic set point rather than a homeostatic one – our comfort zone is stress, not joy. This set point is not easily disrupted.

All four of these factors can be counteracted if we adopt the practice of radical resilience. They are caused by emotional wires and the solution is emotional rewiring. We can use specific, brain-savvy emotional techniques and, to our surprise, feel much better. With repeated use of the techniques, we begin warming up to the idea of processing our emotions, as we associate facing our fears and overcoming them with the positive emotions of resiliency.

As David used EBT, he would realize that he was not left out. He, too, could turn stress into joy. Amazing! Any trace of emotional avoidance would begin to crumble as he experienced that emotional triumph again and again. In time, he would find that high octane emotional processing was an innovative new technology for improving the quality of his daily life.

Also, David was learning non-judgment. He had been successful in business until the financial disaster of Covid, but in romantic relationships, success had eluded him. Sometimes he attributed his relationship challenges to not having met the right person, but mostly, he blamed himself for not being able to get relationships "right."

I said to him, "You get a lot of your relationships right. I'm sure you are loving, kind, creative, and fun with some people."

He said, "Absolutely. I'm great with my nieces and I have really strong relationships with my ex-girlfriends. They see me as a loving, great guy."

"You must have a 'loving, great guy' wire, a resilient circuit, but you probably also have a wire that sends you into another way of being."

He laughed. Humor is core to the method, as, after all, these are just wires!

"Yes, that would be my 'cut and run' wire."

"Exactly. The first step is for you to believe that there is nothing wrong with you. Did anyone tell you that you had a 'cut and run' wire that you could switch off if you processed your wild and woolly emotions?"

"Nope . . . nobody."

"How can you fix something if you don't know what the underlying problem is or how to nullify that problem?"

"Beats me."

"You have all the potential to be an emotional superstar and process your emotions, David. I can show you how to do that."

"Okay. I will stop being so hard on myself – no more judgments. Now . . . show me how to be an emotional superstar."

Chapter 5.

The Antibody: Radical Resilience

David was about to experience radical resilience, switching off a high-stress, very reactive wire, and spiraling up to One. It's resilience under pressure: getting from Brain State 3, 4, or 5 to Brain State 1, quickly and easily. Radical resilience is a core skill for living our best lives, and thinking cannot give it to us. However, processing our full-throttle emotions can!

He could use a series of lead-ins that made it easy for him to turn toxic emotions into healing feelings, with the bonus of switching off that undesirable circuit. Within a few minutes, he would feel present and aware and be ready to move forward effectively with grace and ease. Most important, by taking that action, he would strengthen his resilient wires, thereby boosting his stress antibodies and enhancing his capacity to be spontaneously resilient in the future.

"David, state each lead-in, and before your thinking brain takes over and ruins the process by analyzing it, release your emotions. Start by expressing your anger."

This is usually the most challenging step for people who are new to the method.

"I'm not angry at her. It's my fault. I've never been good at relationships."

"You don't have to be angry with her. You can be angry with the situation. You can be angry with Covid, you can be angry with life. However, anger unlocks the wire. This is not a psychological issue. It is a wiring reset. You can't wire in the new, effective, resilient wire until you break down the old, ineffective, reactive wire. Break open that ridiculous wire! Be bold. Protest what happened!"

"What I am most stressed about is . . . she is so demanding. I feel angry that I am failing at love again, and this keeps on happening to me. Nothing ever changes."

"Be like a lion and roar! Be furious at Lana, at yourself, at Covid, at ANYTHING!"

"I feel angry that . . . Covid is controlling my life. I can't stand it that . . . I finally met a woman . . . a really special woman . . . and I'm acting like an ass."

David paused.

I said, "Fantastic! Keep it up!"

He continued, "I feel ANGRY that . . . she feels lonely. I feel angry that . . . I am working my ass off, and all she can talk about is how lonely she is. Fuck that! What is going on? I HATE it that I don't know what to do. I HATE it that I can't do my job and deal with a relationship. It's too much. How dare she be so demanding? I HATE it that she is so demanding. I HATE it that I am not meeting her needs. I HATE it. I HATE it, I hate it . . ."

"Keep expressing anger until your mind shuts off or you feel sad. Those are the signs that you have fully unlocked the wire, you have released enough stress that your thinking brain is back to functioning well, and you are ready to encourage your emotions to flow from stress to joy. The next lead-in is 'I feel sad that . . .'"

"I'm ready for that . . . I feel sad that . . . she feels alone."

The Resilient Wire

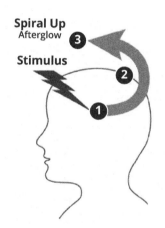

Spiral Up
Afterglow **3**

Stimulus

1
Accurate Emotions
A stimulus enters the brain and we stay connected within, present, and aware. We know what we need.

2
Reasonable Expectations
Unconscious, effective beliefs take charge, decreasing our stress. (e.g., I am worthy, I have power)

3
Effective Response
We take action in ways that meet our needs and enable us to spiral up, honor our purpose, and feel joy.

"Pause and feel the feeling until it fades. Stay connected to the feelings in your body. Wait for words to magically appear in your mind."

"I feel afraid that . . . I am not enough for her."

David paused, extracting all the benefits possible from feeling that emotion.

"The next lead-in is 'I feel guilty that . . .'"

"I don't feel guilty."

"Expressing guilt is the turning point in your flowing feelings. It meets your evolutionary need to find out how you can avoid feeling this stress in the future. Only when we discover how to respond more effectively should this situation arise again does the brain begin filling us with positive emotions. Use the lead-in 'My part of it is . . .' or 'What I could do differently is . . .'"

"My part of it is that . . . I obsess about work and I don't tune in to her feelings."

David paused for a moment, then his entire energy shifted.

"Actually, I do feel grateful. I feel grateful that ... she hasn't left me. I feel happy that . . . I really have feelings for her. I feel secure that . . . I can stop obsessing about work . . . I feel proud that . . . I am changing."

"How do you feel now?"

"Better."

"Let's finish off your dose by creating a plan of action. That will cause your positive emotions to last longer. Say, 'I expect myself to do the best I can to . . .'"

"I expect myself to do the best I can to . . . listen to her and love her."

"What encouragement do you need? What are the positive, powerful words you most need to hear?"

"I need to tell myself: I can do that."

"What is the hard part, the essential pain of life you must face to follow through with that new expectation?"

David said, "That's easy. She could reject me."

"Now reward yourself. Bring to mind the reason you are going to listen to her and love her."

"Intimacy. I want love in my life."

David's words were important, but even more important was his vocal tone. He sounded happy and energetic, bordering on elated. This was a sign that he was at One. He had switched off a reactive neural pathway and activated a resilient neural pathway, and a surge of dopamine and endorphins had been released.

"You did it, David. Wonderful. How do you feel now?"

"The best I have felt since the pandemic began, maybe the best I have felt in years."

He could now bring to Lana something new – himself in his most resilient state of One.

A week later, David called.

I asked, "How can I help?"

He said, "You already did. Something shifted in me during the session. I started opening my heart to Lana, and really listening to her."

"How is your wiring?"

"Better. I'm strengthening those resilient wires. That's my new project."

It's challenging to get started with expressing emotions. At first, the neural pathways of emotional release do not cooperate, but emotional pathways are just brain habits. The more doses of the technique David takes, the more those pathways will become deeper ruts in the road of his emotional brain. He'll access them more easily, and his emotions will flow more rapidly.

He would now become more curious about how to use the method, and as he improved his technique, he would find it useful for stress, but even more, he would notice that he would have some magical moments in his day, every day. That is the gift of the emotional brain.

Part II.
The Solution

Chapter 6.

The Stress Release

You can feel better – much better – in three minutes. In one more minute, you can feel energized and secure that you are moving forward with purpose.

The stress solution is a two-step process. By using these two steps when we are stressed, we can train the brain for radical resilience that is rooted in loving kindness. Stay tenderly aware of your brain state and when you notice that you feel disconnected, negative, or stressed, take a dose to feel better right away, and also, to take care of your health.

During a course on EBT for medical students, Michael Merzenich, the father of neuroplasticity, spoke about training the brain for resilience, saying, "If the brain is ever to be cured of any condition, it will not be chemical. It will be by training. The brain basically has to train itself out of its problems to the best of its ability, because only in that way can the training be complete and natural enough to confer strong resilience against future relapse."

If resiliency training is so central to natural and sustainable health, then the procedure is worth doing well. Early in developing the tools, I discovered that if the technique was not really clear and precise, the lizard brain would find a way to sabotage our success in rewiring old ineffective neural pathways and encoding new effective ones. We found ways to outsmart the reptilian brain and incorporated them into the method you can learn now.

As you experiment with using the technique, expect resistance from the reptilian brain. That resistance may show up as assuring yourself that everyone else can express emotions, but somehow you will be the one person who cannot learn how. Your brain is like a muscle. Use your emotional muscle and you'll strengthen it. Each time you take a dose, your brain opens up more. Your brain becomes more emotionally fluid.

What if you are highly thinking-oriented? If we have not been taught early in life that emotions are safe, and that we can express them, then the most common way to process life is to overuse cognitive functioning. We think way too much. We suppress our emotions and become really good problem solvers, which makes people around us very happy. We can solve their problems. This is why so many highly successful people do not discover EBT until mid-life or after, when they have succeeded in every other realm of life. Everything goes very well except the aspects of life that are dependent upon our being emotional superstars: love and health. These become high priorities later in life.

For example, Deena was a senior vice president of a major brokerage firm and took early retirement at age 55. She was so talented that she could fix almost any problem and she had been paid handsomely for it. By retiring early, she had expected to travel the world with friends. Then a shelter-in-place order was placed on her community in mid-March of 2020. She couldn't buy clothes, go to concerts, travel, or do anything but stay home, water her plants, and come to terms with who she was and what she wanted from life.

Deena said, "I have no idea how to process my emotions. I was raised by a mother who fed me sweets while ridiculing me for being fat and an alcoholic father who ignored me. I had no tools to process all that stress, and built on my strength: thinking. That strategy made me more successful than my wildest dreams, but now I want success in other areas. I've never had a satisfying relationship and my weight has become a health issue."

The first week that Deena began learning the emotional techniques, she was flummoxed, and said, "I can't learn this. I am past my prime and I've never been good at emotions."

I said, "Your emotional brain is perfectly capable of processing emotions. You have beautiful resiliency pathways in your brain. All you are doing is making them strong, like ruts in the road. Each time you use the technique, it deepens those ruts."

By the second week, she had almost quit, but something inside her would not give up. During the third week, she had a turnaround.

She said, "I stopped trying so hard. I stated the lead-ins and didn't judge myself. I felt compassion for myself. Then, using the technique started becoming an adventure. I was curious about what words would appear in my mind, and then my emotions started coming up. Now I feel so much lighter and full of hope. I can do this!"

The key to seeing important results early in the process is using specific words (lead-ins). When the brain is in stress, switching out of it requires several small steps taken in a specific order. The words have been carefully crafted and they will help you find your brain's hidden resiliency pathway even when you are stressed out. With each lead-in, you move along that pathway toward a state of connection and well-being.

A small group of professors met weekly for several years, learning the tools. One of them was a psychiatrist. Her use of the tools was particularly riveting because she seemed to savor each lead-in. After one session, I asked her how she would coach someone new to EBT. She paused for a very long time, then said, "Trust the tools."

Trust in the tools builds each time you use them, but using them is very simple. State the words, then pause. That is the hardest part. By pausing and turning your attention to your body, and waiting for another few seconds, your emotional brain will reward you. It will bubble up some words that immediately ring true. Right in that moment, when the words arise from your unconscious mind and appear in your conscious mind, your stress will ease. You'll feel more connected to yourself.

How often do you take doses of EBT? Whenever you feel disconnected or stressed, take a dose. Some people set reminders for times during the day when they know they are apt to be stressed. Others set reminders at regular intervals throughout the day. You can memorize the lead-ins, but there is a mobile app for the method, which makes using the techniques easier. The app is designed to take the guesswork out of using all the tools. I recommend using it so you can take small doses whenever you want and find it easier to use the techniques.

This is the EBT tool designed to relieve situational stress. There are other tools that enable you to focus on rewiring specific wires, both survival circuits and core circuits. However, this tool has an indirect effect on these circuits, and using it is the best way to launch your EBT practice.

Each of the three steps takes about a minute, but you can take less or more time, depending upon what your brain seems to need at the time. Trust your natural inclinations. Sometimes you'll want to talk about the situation for more than one minute. You may feel complete and satisfied after expressing only three to six angers.

Typically, the whole process of releasing emotions and creating an action plan takes two to five minutes.

Most people give themselves a dose about five times per day, but when you begin, your reptilian brain might be a bit "snappish" and resist using it. You might even only use it once per day for a while. As using these neural pathways becomes more comfortable for your lizard brain, you'll naturally want to use it more. If you're not having fun using the tools, then push back for a while and remind yourself, "If it's not fun, it's not EBT." If your brain resists using the tools, give it what it really wants, which is emotional connection. Find one person or more with whom to use the tools or find connections and support on the ebt.org website.

What follow are the lead-ins for the stress solution along with ideas about how to use it in highly effective ways right from the start.

Minute #1
Talk About the Situation

The situation is . . .
What I am most stressed about is . . .

Minute #2
Express Healthy Anger

I feel angry that . . .
I can't stand it that . . .
I hate it that . . .

Minute #3
Negative Emotions Become Positive

I feel sad that . . .
I feel afraid that . . .
I feel guilty that . . .
I feel grateful that . . .
I feel happy that . . .
I feel secure that . . .
I feel proud that . . .

Now, let's look more closely at how to take a dose of the stress vaccine . . .

Minute #1
Talk About the Situation

It's probably no surprise that talking about what's bothering us launches the stress solution. By beginning to tell the story of our upset, we activate just the errant wires that are taking a simple everyday stressor and causing it to eat at us, put us on edge, or trigger cravings.

This takes one minute only, and if you can allow just a full minute for the process, you will both zero in on the wire that is causing the problem and keep from releasing so much stress that you prevent the natural rewiring benefits you could get from the process. There are two lead-ins for the first step in releasing stress.

The situation is . . .

State the lead-in, then talk about what is bothering you. The key here is to state the facts only. Do not state feelings. You are targeting what is causing you stress and consulting the bottom of your brain where the circuits of toxic stress reside. Expressing emotions at this point reduces the stress you need to activate a wire, takes you out of contact with these extreme circuits, and scatters your opportunity to assertively and soundly shut them off. We need to be clear about what is bothering us to start the process of positive emotional neuroplasticity. After about 20 to 40 seconds, you will notice that you feel complete and that you have adequately described what you're stressed about because you will naturally pause. Continue that pause until you feel connected to your body. During that time, your unconscious mind will organize around the circuit you have activated.

What I am most stressed about is . . .

After describing the stressful situation, pause for long enough to reappraise your upset. This pause has a balancing effect. If your stress activation is extreme, it quiets down slightly, and if it is milder, then bringing up the most stressful aspect of the situation will increase your stress level. There is a certain grace in the simplicity of this process. If stress is too high, the prefrontal cortex will not function effectively enough to use the tool, and if it is too low, we will miss out on rewiring the reactive circuits that cause the most mayhem. Instead, the brain is now readied for processing just the emotions that it can most efficiently process to release stress and build neural pathways of radical resilience.

This is a remarkably easy step with one caveat: we must release control. With an ounce of emotional surrender, the brain will bubble up to consciousness the specific part of that stressful situation that it has enough functionality to process and that is the most harmful to you. Effectively clearing the most harmful aspect is a natural survival characteristic.

The key is to allow the wisdom of your emotional brain to inform you of what bothers you the most. Do not use your thinking brain to analyze what you're most stressed about. Instead, state the lead-in and pause. Turn your attention to your body. Wait for several words to appear in your mind.

Keep your topic statement brief. Be factual and include only one topic. For example, "I could have Covid," rather than "There is a chance I could have Covid and I could be infecting my co-workers and family." Use very basic language because the wire we want to switch off is in the most primitive part of the brain, the part of us that functions at ages one to four. If you use abstract terms and complex concepts, you're probably not tapping into these primitive areas. What if the words that bubble up are not brief and on a single topic? Just pause. When you feel connected again, state the lead-in once more. It's likely that a simple, singular topic will appear in your mind.

At age 19, Heather was so enthusiastic and bright that she could hardly contain the tumble of words she was expressing as she began. In stress, most of us go to extremes, including talking, either being incredibly cryptic, keeping it to so few words that it's hard to know what is bothering us, or releasing a flood of words. This structured approach keeps us in the mid-range. If we talk about our situation too much, so much stress is released that we have a great story to tell but have missed our opportunity to use strong negative emotions to rewire the very cause of the situation. In other words, we found a way to feel better for the moment but did not rewire the circuit that was triggering the problem.

I coached Heather through her first use of the tool. Coaching involves intruding upon her process, as these self-regulatory circuits are primitive and survival-based. It is far more effective to jump in and interrupt the process than to reflect on the process later on. Emotional wires are that strong and slippery!

She said, "The situation is . . . I am completely devastated and feel so angry at my parents. I am living with them and my 10-year-old sister, and I am so angry . . ."

"Heather, great start, except, please circle back. State the facts, no feelings, for the best effect."

She went on, "The situation is . . . I am home from college and my parents are both nurses and they are gone long hours. They are completely stressed and I am at home with Maggie. She misses her friends and is addicted to sugar and videogames. I know that my parents are exhausted but Maggie is being neglected."

She paused, connected with herself, then said, "What I am most stressed about is . . . Maggie is hurting."

For Heather to talk about the problem and identify the topic took about 40 seconds. Again, the timing does not matter as much as honoring the responses in your body. When your emotional brain is complete with this step, you'll have a sense in your body that you are "done." Your words will stop flowing, and this is the sign that you are on your brain's resiliency pathway and ready for the next step.

Minute #2
Express Healthy Anger

Continue your stress solution by expressing anger about the situation. This fulfills two needs. First, the initial expression of anger can help you access the more primitive areas of your brain. The brain is a storehouse of wires that bring past experiences forward in time, and those that cause the most stress are the ones that were encoded when the reptilian brain was dominant. It's those wires that we want to roust out and unlock so we can weaken and, over time, reconsolidate them. The more outrage we can express, the more productive the tool.

Also, by expressing anger, we release stress, and that release returns the thinking brain to improved top-down self-regulatory functioning over the bottom-up reactive wires in the emotional brain. There are three lead-ins for this step in the process.

I feel angry that . . . I can't stand it that . . . I hate it that . . .

These three lead-ins give us a way to ensure that anger is both safe and effective. The lead-ins are graduated so that low-intensity anger launches the process, followed by two more that elicit more extreme and unbalanced anger. You are protesting the situation, keeping your emotional expressions on the topic.

Be sure to add expletives, if you are comfortable with them, as a way to boost your effectiveness. Anger unlocks the resiliency pathway and enables you to experience tender, healing negative emotions that flow into positive feelings.

If, at any time, you sense that this is not safe for you, then, by all means, stop using it. When you initially use it and find it uncomfortable, this is normal. The reptile is not happy, but you will win it over in time and with practice.

The anger skill is core to the prevention of anxiety and depression and to the success of expressing tender and healing sadness followed by balanced and calming fear. This is because a brief, bold expression of anger shifts us out of a toxic stress state. Without that physiological shift, the sadness Heather would express in the third minute of the process would turn into depression, powerlessness, or self-pity. That expression of her feelings could actually amplify her stress rather than diminish it. The same is true for anxiety. Heather would find herself expressing such intense fear that she would have a chance of retraumatizing herself.

As Heather transitioned into minute #2 of using the stress solution, I said, "Be gentle with yourself. Nudge yourself to express healthy, bold A+ Anger. Protest being harmed! You do not need to blame anyone or shame yourself. Just focus on this situation. What about it do you want to protest?"

Heather drew a blank.

"Anger is really hard for me."

"Take it slowly then. Sometimes it is hard because early in life, we experienced unhealthy anger – rage, hostility, or even aggression. Or, if nobody expressed anger in our family, we would have no idea that it was normal to feel angry. The brain gives us the emotion of anger to protest being harmed, but it can take time and practice for the unconscious mind to perceive that healthy anger is a good thing."

"Nobody ever seems angry in my family. Everything is exceedingly calm on the surface, but underneath all that, I have felt uneasy and sensed that something was missing or swept under the rug. I caught their suppressed emotions, which is why I am the one in the family that is the 'overly sensitive one' and the person with the social anxiety disorder."

"That must have been hard. I'm sorry."

Heather said, "Thanks. How can this be easier?"

"Use the lead-ins. Wait to see what bubbles up. The words of the lead-ins themselves activate the emotions. Circle around to the last lead-in, which was: 'What I am most stressed about is . . . Maggie is hurting.' Stay on this topic going forward."

"I feel angry that . . . Maggie is hurting . . . I can't stand it that . . . Maggie is hurting . . . I HATE it that . . . my parents don't make her a priority. I'm furious that our family is so messed up. I HATE it that I don't know what to do about it. I am furious that they don't give a damn about her. I HATE THAT. I HATE IT. I HATE IT. I HATE IT!!!!"

Heather had accomplished a great deal. Instead of bumping up against toxic emotions and abandoning herself, she had been determined and had stayed securely connected to her emotions. She had expressed A+ Anger that was bold, powerful, safe, on topic, and healing. Her thinking brain was now back online . . .

What was the next step? It was to move along her resiliency pathway, boost her stress antibodies, and activate a dopamine and endorphin rush.

Minute #3
Negative Emotions Become Positive

The next step in releasing stress is to complete seven sentences. Each one will guide you in expressing a feeling, first three negative emotions, then four positive ones.

The major benefit of the first two steps is that when we turn our attention to expressing emotions, they are often quite magical. The feelings shimmer and you can feel them all through your body. If we had not taken the first two steps, these feelings would be dry. They would be glorified thoughts, without the passion and body arousal that make emotions so glorious. A thought alone is flat, but emotions are multilayered. We might just label a feeling but miss the added enlivening benefit of allowing it to flow through our bodies. That is when the magic happens.

Each of the seven feelings that flow now has a unique role in the process.

Sadness is the first emotion to arise after anger has been cleared. Sadness is distinct from depression as it arises from a higher brain state and is tender and healing. Only one deep sadness statement is typically needed to feel complete, but if you need more, then express more. Often if you have really let loose with your anger, there will only be one deep, tender sadness to express. However, as always, use the tool in a way that feels good to you. If it feels good, it will benefit your brain's resiliency pathways.

Sadness helps us grieve the loss, and although we can use many sadness statements, there is a special benefit to expressing only one. Knowing that we only use one sadness statement gives us encouragement to focus deeper within and discover what we are most sad about. When we discover that and express it, we know ourselves better. Pausing at that point to feel that feeling until it fades clears the stress more rapidly and enables us to grieve the most important loss of this situation.

I coached Heather through her flow of feelings.

"Focus on the lead-in. Do not think your way through this. Just clear your mind by pausing and then focus on saying, 'I feel sad that . . .' Pause and wait for words to appear. They will come from your unconscious mind and will elicit feelings of tenderness and compassion for yourself."

Heather said, "I feel sad that . . ."

She paused, turning her attention to her body, tolerating irresolution, so that the words that appeared in her mind would be short and choppy. This would be an indication that she had unlocked a very deep circuit, as the reptilian brain's messages are primitive. Long statements often come from the neocortex, which is not helpful, and actually shuts off the natural resiliency flow of the emotional brain.

Heather continued, "I feel sad that . . . my sister is sad."

"Nicely done. If you can possibly do this, avoid saying anything. Just focus on your feeling. Feel it until it fades. Extract from that sadness all the healing and tenderness that you can."

I could hear her breathing, which was calm and deep.

Then after a few seconds, she said, "It faded. My sadness faded, and now I feel . . . fear."

The process is universal as this natural flow of feelings starts with anger, then moves into sadness, then fear, and finally, guilt. The progression causes the emotions to become unstuck, and their order mirrors the way we grieve, learn, change, and grow. It protects us from finding ourselves in stuck, toxic emotions.

"That's the next lead-in: 'I feel afraid that . . .'"

With our stress hormones cleared, we can feel our fear. If we had focused on fear earlier, we would have gotten in touch with distorted fear, which is terror. Now, we can find the true threat, face that fear, and allow the feeling to fade. The fear will lose its power over us.

Heather said, "I feel afraid that . . . what I'm most afraid of is . . . Maggie will be . . ."

She paused for a moment, then realized that the words did not ring true. Then she said the lead-in again.

"I feel afraid that . . . Maggie is going to feel like I felt at that age: abandoned."

"Feel that fear. Let it flow through your body. The part that is fueled by stress will fade so you will feel more secure about the true threat."

She breathed deeply three more times, then the fear faded.

Heather continued, "I feel guilty that . . . nothing is coming up. I'm drawing a blank. I hate this feeling. I quit!"

"Good limits. You can always stop. If you think it isn't working or don't like what is happening, then stop."

"Laurel, can't you make this easier for me?"

"Okay, try the lead-in, 'my part of this is . . .'"

Always personalize the lead-ins when your emotional

brain becomes snappish and does its best to shut down the process.

"My part of it is . . . I feel guilty that . . . I obsess about Maggie's happiness. I want her to have zero pain . . . forever!"

"Check your body. Does that ring true?"

Heather paused and said, "Yes, that rings true."

Then she burst out laughing.

"Laurel, that's ridiculous. Nobody can protect another person from all life's pain. I don't even know if having a pain-free life would be good for Maggie or anyone else!"

From the moment she identified her guilt statement, the reactive circuits of unreasonable expectations would be updating their neural connections. Without direct action, her brain, through experiential learning, would begin to change the wires unlocked by stress in favor of reasonable expectations that strengthen her resilient wires.

She paused until she felt connected again and continued with the lead-ins: "I feel grateful that . . . I love my sister . . . I feel happy that . . . we are sheltering in place together . . . I feel secure that . . . I am a good sister to her . . . I feel proud that . . . I didn't quit . . . and I am expressing my emotions!"

"You did it! How do you feel now?"

"I'm at One. I feel a glow in my body. I feel joy."

Heather had released her stress. She was in the ideal state for the second step in the process, moving forward with clarity and purpose . . .

Chapter 7.

The Power Booster

Imagine yourself looking out at the ocean on a beautiful day, and pausing to breathe in the fresh air. You are at Brain State 1 and what's important is that you savor that moment and enjoy all its chemical effects.

That's precisely what works best after you've cleared away stress and spiraled up to a better state. Pause for a moment and enjoy your bliss. Savor it!

In a moment or two, the bliss will fade, as your mind will turn to taking your next step. This is a pivotal moment as we can use that bliss to change the course of our day, but without the benefit of a slight bit of structure, we may return to old ways, and miss that opportunity.

The challenge is to make that plan by using your whole brain. We need to consult the wisdom of the emotional brain with its trillions of neural connections that give us insight, a gut feel, and a profound "knowing" of what is right for us. With this technique, the Take Action Tool, you can do that.

Just complete each of four lead-ins. For each one, turn your attention to your body, and wait for some words to bubble up into your mind. If you do that, most of the time, the words will tell you your next step forward. They will reflect the truths your emotional brain has extracted from all of your experiences of life.

You can double-check the wisdom of those words easily, as we have an innate approach and avoidance system. If the words bubble up and you have the body feel of "Yes, that's right! That rings true!" then you have nailed it. That is a wise next step. If they do not ring true, that's not a problem. Take an extra few seconds and repeat the lead-in until words come to mind that do feel right to you. Trust your body and the tools. You'll second-guess yourself less and make smart decisions more quickly and easily.

This process is enormously effective no matter what you're considering. It could be whether or not to have another baby or whether to shower now or later. However, keep in mind that what bubbles up from the unconscious mind may be completely illogical, but if it rings true, it will be brilliant. So, be expansive and creative as you use the technique and always expect some surprises!

Today I was facilitating a telegroup and a group member, George, spoke up. He said that he had been in total stress overload the night before. His family had been evacuated from their home due to wildfires in the area. This added to his already significant stress from remote-schooling his two children while trying to take customer service calls for his job.

George said, "I processed my emotions, but my mind wouldn't shut off."

I was surprised because the second step of the process

typically calms us down, no matter what.

I asked, "Did you use the Take Action Tool?"

He paused, then responded, "No, I forgot to use it."

"You can use it now if you like. Just imagine yourself in bed last night with your mind refusing to shut off. Then use the tool."

George said, "Okay . . . I can imagine . . ."

"Just use the lead-ins and notice the words that appear in your mind."

"I expect myself to do the best I can to . . . accept that my mind is going to race for as long as it chooses to race."

"How is that?"

"It rings true. It sounds right to me. My body is telling me that it's a green light. I can go with this one."

"Now give yourself some encouragement."

"My positive powerful thought . . . I can do that. The essential pain is . . ."

At that moment, George let out a gasp.

". . . I am not in complete control. My earned reward is . . . vibrancy."

"How was that for you?"

"I'm surprised! My thinking brain would never have created such a perfect plan, one that made my body completely relax. I get it. My power to know what is true for me is in my emotional brain."

The expectation did not have to make sense. For George's stress response to switch off, all he had to do was bring to mind his precise need based on the complicated person he was in the complicated life he was living. That's the forte of the emotional brain. Not only do the words bubble up from it, but they give us an instant reading of whether it is right or not, along with a burst of dopamine to motivate us.

In Heather's situation, she could use the technique to sustain her positive emotions and help her decide how to connect with her parents and Maggie.

I asked her, "How are you feeling now?"

She said, "Good, 2-ish, not quite how I felt a few moments ago."

"What do you need?"

"I need to stop thinking so much. My mind went right to what I was missing out on when my friends were doing stuff, and what I should do about school, and whether or not I should talk with my parents about how worried I am about Maggie. Now I'm at 3 or 4, or maybe I'm at 10. I don't know what I need."

"You need the Take Action Tool."

"Okay, I'll do it."

"Great, it has four lead-ins. After using it you will know just what is right for you to do, and you'll feel rewarded for doing it."

She said, "Show me how to use this Take Action Tool. I think I need it."

I said, "Will do."

The four lead-ins of this technique form a neural pathway that we construct when we are at Brain State 1 and accessing all our wires of wise judgment. Then, when stressful moments arise, we can activate that wire and have confidence that we know our plan and are charged up to use it. Procrastination? That stops. So does indecisiveness. Enjoy this jewel of a technique.

Minute #4
Take Action With Purpose

I expect myself to do the best I can to . . .
My positive, powerful thought . . .
The essential pain is . . .
My earned reward is . . .

Let's focus on each of the four lead-ins so that you can use them to move forward with clarity and purpose. This is not hard. You can do this. Just use the lead-ins and your emotional brain will lead the way.

Minute #4
Take Action With Purpose

After we release stress, we feel complete. Pause for a moment and enjoy that feeling. Then continue to the first step of the Take Action Tool. It is to identify what you expect of yourself, something reasonable that is neither too harsh nor too easy.

Your expectation can take any form that gives you a guide to moving forward, and takes you up and over the stressed state to connection and well-being. For example, the expectation can be about your own internal process, such as being as stressed as you want to be or being compassionate and gentle with yourself. Any expectation can be nurturing and effective if it reflects what you actually need to evolve.

Finding that reasonable expectation is remarkably easy. Again, trust your body. As you enjoy this fourth minute of the technique, after you have released stress, you are often at One. In that brain state, you know intuitively what is the right next step for you. Still to this day, when I launch into stating one of the lead-ins of this tool, I feel slightly apprehensive. Will words actually arrive in my mind to complete the sentence? Sometimes I have to take several deep breaths, and feel a wave of love for myself, but then the words appear. Magic! Use each of the four lead-ins and pause, waiting for just the right words to bubble up to your conscious mind. With each lead-in, your clarity increases and the technique finishes with the flourish of your purpose for following through.

It is all so easy. No more overthinking!

I expect myself to do the best I can to . . .

The initial lead-in takes the most courage. We do not know for sure what we expect of ourselves. There is a multitude of possibilities. It's essential to do the best we can but to stop short of neglecting or abusing ourselves.

How do we figure that out? We don't. We let the wisdom of our emotional brain complete the sentence. The added words "do the best I can to" make that reverence for ourselves explicit.

Becoming comfortable with your emotional brain means using your thinking brain to be a responsive parent to yourself. Most of us didn't get all our needs met as children, and the relationship with those who raised us becomes internalized. To reset that relationship with ourselves, we are very careful to be warm and loving to ourselves. We both nurture ourselves and set effective limits. This approach of having a highly warm, loving relationship with ourselves that is neither permissive nor depriving is that reset.

Any healing experience begins with love, so this technique incorporates the practice of loving ourselves unconditionally. Anytime a reactive wire is ruling us, the stress hormones cause judgment, rigidity, and perfectionism. Out goes unconditional love. You will not be asking yourself to be loving to yourself when your stress chemicals make that impossible. Instead, the first three minutes of the technique involve switching off those stress chemicals and making it biologically realistic to feel love for yourself again.

In raising my children, we had a family saying, "The tight fist of overcontrol!" The concept is that when we believe that we have to do everything perfectly, we go into overcontrol, and expectations become overly harsh. We have to be perfect. Instead, it's more effective to loosen that tight fist of overcontrol and know that we do not have to be perfect to be wonderful. When we push an extra percent as if all that matters is getting it right, no love or creativity can find their way into our hearts. Instead, we open our hand to doing the very best we can do and no more. Overcontrol stops, and we have more vibrancy and freedom in our lives.

When Heather heard that she should trust her gut and not push herself to do everything perfectly, she said, "I have worked my whole life to be perfect. You are telling me that I should slack off?"

"I'm telling you to connect with yourself and do the very best you can, stopping short of neglecting or abusing yourself."

She said, "I know how to indulge myself and how to deprive myself, but nothing in between."

"This technique will help you find the pathway forward that is right for you. By using it you will discover expectations that enable you to strive for excellence within what is realistic for you at that time. You will learn to trust the tools only one way – by using them."

"Okay, I'll try it."

My positive, powerful thought . . .

Once you have established a reasonable expectation, pause again, connect with yourself to ensure you stay at

Brain State 1, and say the next lead-in, which is rather strange. It's "My positive, powerful thought . . ."

The act of stating a new reasonable expectation is novel and outside of the reptilian brain's comfort zone, which is to repeat old patterns. This is a problem because if the stress chemicals take over, we're back to the reactive wire calling the shots, with our thinking brain finding every reason to obsess, ruminate, self-doubt, or procrastinate. We need to switch off that stress, so by adding a few positive, powerful words, we quiet the reptile.

Choose any words you like, and don't rush this! As you discover the encouraging words you most need to hear (e.g., "I can do that!"), the brain has plenty of time to bring up an image of yourself doing it. The experience is like seeing yourself on video doing precisely what you intend to do, even though you haven't taken one step in that direction yet. The image forms a neural circuit, so your brain is fully prepared with a pathway for moving forward.

Also, the last two steps of the technique require precision in understanding and accepting what is difficult for you to do to follow through and choosing the reward that is so powerful in your inner chemical landscape that you would gladly do that difficult thing. Having that mental image in place makes the last two lead-ins bring you an authentic response that busts you past procrastination, rebellion, stalls, and resistance!

The essential pain is . . .

With that vision of ourselves being the victor and moving forward, we can become aware of the hard part for us in following through. This is important, as any

83

reasonable expectation requires us to grow, change, and evolve, which means facing the difficult part – the downside – and surrendering to learning the lessons that enable us to evolve. In EBT, there are seven essential pains of life.

The 7 Essential Pains

- **I am alone.**
- **I am not perfect.**
- **I am not in complete control.**
- **It takes work.**
- **Some people may reject me.**
- **I must receive.**
- **I must give.**

These are the seven core essential pains of the method but do not limit yourself to them. If the words that appear in your mind to complete the sentence after the lead-in ring true for you, they are correct. This personalizes the method to fit your brain and your needs.

Facing this essential pain takes away its power to get us stuck and paves the way for us to fully experience the reward of following through. Pause and feel the essential pain until your emotions and body sensations fade, then use the last lead-in to reward yourself.

My earned reward is . . .

As the emotions from being aware of the essential pain of following through fade, turn your attention to the reward. The reward must be more rewarding than the pain is painful. If it is not, circle back around and begin again. Otherwise, state the reward, and you'll feel the glow.

Say, "My earned reward is ..." and again, wait for words to appear in your mind. In EBT, which is based on Erikson's developmental theory modified to reflect neuroscience and our program research, there are seven earned rewards in life.

The 7 Rewards

- **Sanctuary – peace & power from within**
- **Authenticity – feeling whole & being genuine**
- **Vibrancy – healthy with a zest for life**
- **Integrity – doing the right thing**
- **Intimacy – giving & receiving love**
- **Spirituality – the grace, beauty & mystery of life**
- **Freedom – common excesses fade**

All of these rewards are meaningful, but you must choose the one that is most important to you in the moment, the one that causes you to feel rewarded even though you are doing hard things. It's by setting an expectation high enough so that it is challenging (the brain loves us to challenge ourselves) and then holding a thought of the higher reward that matters most to you that you can follow through with pride and joy

Bring to mind the rewards and notice which of them is met with the most significant body sensations and emotions. That is your earned reward. Feel the surge of joy it elicits and pause to savor your state of inner peace and power.

When Heather released her stress, she said, "I feel guilty that I obsess about Maggie's happiness. I want her to have zero pain . . . forever!" and went on to express her positive emotions of love and caring for Maggie . . . but the real learning and Heather's security in how to move forward would require using an additional tool.

Heather said, "I expect myself to do the best I can to . . . I don't know. I can never decide anything. Now, this is really stressing me."

"Your job is to warmly observe yourself and give yourself unconditional love no matter what. That's the sign of an emotionally healthy adult. You can do that! Accept yourself as you are. That is the foundation for astonishing effectiveness in life. Use a process expectation like, 'I expect myself to be as indecisive as I need to be for as long as I need to be.'"

"Okay, I'll use that. My positive, powerful thought . . . I have the power to do that . . . and the essential pain, the hard part for me, is . . . I am not perfect."

"My earned reward is . . ."

"My earned reward is . . . authenticity, feeling whole and being genuine."

With each cycle through her feelings and resetting of her expectations, Heather would update the out-of-date or ambiguous expectations in her reactive wires. We are not in complete control of how much our wires will change, sometimes slightly, and often when we least expect it, radically.

I said, "You can sit with the feelings you have now, as feeling your emotions after giving yourself a dose of EBT is associated with updating the wire."

For Brook to stay connected to her feelings is the first step toward replacing that faulty old wire with a new and effective one. The objective in using the tools is to erase the old wire. This is called reconsolidation, the only way of treating these wires that has produced lasting results. Coping by avoiding triggers, encoding new wires of healthy habits without rewiring the hefty reactive wires that compete with them ("extinction"), or using positive thinking does not erase the old wire. Hard-won changes may be less likely to last.

Each time a reactive wire is activated by stress, it is open to rewiring. Change in the wire occurs from experiential learning. You can't think your way to updating the wire. It takes activating it and being aware of your feelings when it is unlocked. That incorporates the new message into the neural circuit. The dopamine from positive emotions locks in the synaptic connections for improved retention of the new memory.

For example, after using this technique, for a period of two to six hours, Heather's reactive wiring will be unlocked and labile, with the changes in it still fragile. Then, while she sleeps that night, her hippocampus will store the updated circuit into long-term memory ("long-term potentiation"). This is the way updated unconscious memories become lasting. The memory becomes permanent until it is activated and updated again. This reconsolidating or updating of wires is the basis for EBT and building stress immunity, raising our set point, and achieving spontaneous radical resilience.

I told her to make another pass through the tool when she felt energized and drawn to using it again.

She said, "I want to do another one now. I think this

is complicated by how I feel about my sister, my parents, and . . ."

"Great. Do a quick and easy release and see where it takes you . . ."

Heather launched into it: "The situation is . . . my parents are doing the best they can, and so is my sister, and so am I, but the whole situation is so strange. I'm not sure they know how stressed she is. They are worried enough about being infected with Covid, and I don't want to worry them even more."

"What I am most stressed about is . . ."

"What I'm most stressed about is . . . I don't want to worry my parents."

"Put your thinking brain back online with some healthy anger."

"I feel angry that . . . I'm so scared to hurt them. I can't stand it that . . . I don't know what to do . . . I HATE it that . . . I am in this spot. I HATE IT!!!! Which makes me sad. I feel sad that . . . I don't know what to do . . . I feel afraid that . . . I will make the wrong decision . . . I feel guilty that . . . I am not telling them the truth about how I feel."

Her voice warmed and she said, "Something shifted."

"Great, you're riding your resilient circuit now. Go ahead and spiral up."

"I feel grateful that . . . I figured this out. I feel happy that . . . I'm already making a plan. I feel secure that . . . I am doing the right thing, and I feel PROUD that . . . I am going to tell them the truth."

"Go ahead with your Take Action Tool."

"I expect myself to do the best I can to . . . speak up and tell my parents the situation with Maggie. My positive, powerful thought . . . It's not that hard. The essential pain . . . It takes work. My earned reward is . . . integrity."

By rifling through her feelings in complicated, high-stakes situations, Heather was evolving, just the way we all can from the enormous stress of responding to the coronavirus pandemic. That last dose of EBT required Heather about two minutes of focused emotional effort. She not only strengthened her stress antibodies but also experienced rewards that one cannot buy – only earn by flexing our emotional muscles.

In a world in which there are very real social, emotional, and physical dangers, we are hiding more and more. Some of that is the essential pain of life, but Heather won't know when to speak up and when to be quiet until she connects to the deepest part of herself, at Brain State 1. In that state, the wires from past experiences when she used good judgment will be online, and the extremes of Brain State 5, with its all-or-nothing responses, will be offline.

By learning to "get to One" before moving forward, she will learn that there is no shortcut to processing life. It can be difficult, and it takes as many doses of the technique as it takes to get there. This practice will teach Heather the skills of tolerating irresolution and building emotional honesty with herself.

These are the two steps of the stress vaccine. Using it the first time can be a little scary, but by the third time, you'll love using it! Don't wait. Start feeling the immense joy of emotional resilience now!

Part III.
Radical Resilience

Chapter 8.
Sustain Your Immunity:
The 7 Rewards

There is tremendous power in those times when we feel miserable, then do the little emotional dance of EBT, and feel great. That experience brings inner security, and a new sense of peace from within.

That immediate shift in brain state gives us momentary control and relief, but not lasting immunity. It's chronic stress that is the health issue. Instead of a flash-in-the-pan happy moment, we need a way to feel better faster and also to avoid the chronic stress trap.

Evolution delivered a way to do that. Using the prefrontal cortex, we can focus our attention on why we do what we do, and if that matches up with the survival of the species, like caring for our young or doing right by our neighbor, that thought is shuttled down to the emotional brain. There, in our reward center (made up of the nucleus accumbens and septal area), it activates neurotransmitters, and positive emotions flow. That switches off the sympathetic nervous system that triggers stress and activates the parasympathetic nervous system of relaxation. Joy swamps stress.

This power of positive emotions to overcome stress was recognized as far back as the 17th century. Philosopher and, some say, early father of neuroscience, Benito Spinoza proposed that the only hope for switching off a negative emotion was to overpower it with a stronger positive one.

The complex relationship between stress and positive emotions has been obscured by the growing pains of psychological theories that have not been brain-based. Sigmund Freud's focus was on the emotional brain, but he never mentioned emotions like joy and gratitude, and the behaviorists focus on thoughts and behaviors, not emotions. It was Martin Seligman in 1998 who chose positive psychology as the theme of his American Psychological Association presidency. His leadership moved psychology toward rewards of purpose, a positive step. Research conducted by Richard Davidson during the 1990s garnered support for the neural bases of emotion promoting human flourishing, including meditation and related contemplative practices. The mindfulness movement followed.

There is only one caveat regarding the power of emotions: when stress-reactive wires are in charge, we cannot feel them, but only by shutting off the stress response can positive emotions flow. Until recently, we didn't know how to use emotional techniques to switch off the stress response quickly. Now that we have the option to take a few doses of EBT and switch off stress arousal, we can rely more on the power of positive emotions. Instead of a stress activation becoming stuck on for hours or days, we can see it as an arc, beginning with stress and ending with joy. What's more, the stress segment of the arc is essential to optimal health because it is only when we are stress-activated that we update our old expectations to current realities. What a perfect process! Get triggered, update our wiring, and spiral up to a natural high.

Was that what evolutionary biology intended? What if chronic stress was not on the agenda after all, and instead was an unintended consequence of modern life, which we failed to spot earlier? What if the truth was all along that the stress response was something far bigger than the fight-or-flight response – a "joy response"? In this model, stress is a pit stop – a state where we stop briefly for wiring repairs, breaking up outdated beliefs, and receiving some spiritual energy – before continuing on our pathway to a higher state of being.

Now that we have new emotional technology and can switch off stress more rapidly when we are in allostasis, it makes sense to focus on the positive. We are always on our way back to joy.

Perhaps all along, our genes have been striving to return us to joy. Theologians, mystics, and poets have spoken of that emotional journey over the ages. It turns out that they were right, and we can think differently about stress.

Now we can tell ourselves a new story: Instead of girding ourselves against an impending stressful event and being riddled with fear, even as we wonder how our post-Covid world will be, we can feel confident. We know we have that joy response inside us. Yes, we will feel bad at times, but then, once again, as we connect with our emotional and spiritual core, that internal protective joy response clicks in. It creates a safety net, so we ride the wave of evolutionary biology, which wants us to reestablish optimal physiology and well-being.

This is a back-to-basics approach. We can use the stress vaccine to encode the joy response and radically expand our potential to do good. We are accustomed to discovering new levels of excellence in other arenas. For example, SpaceX was recently launched to take NASA astronauts Bob Behnken and Doug Hurley into orbit. This represents the first time NASA astronauts had flown on US rockets since the end of the space shuttle program a decade ago. According to the NASA deputy administrator Jim Morhard, "We're at the dawn of a new age."

What about the dawn of a new age of pushing the limits on our emotional and spiritual lives? We don't even have to get on one of those spaceflights. Instead, we can face new frontiers in the orbit within. We can get triggered by stress, then with only a moment of recognition ("Hey, I'm stressed!"), plow through our emotions and find ourselves spiraling up to a state of peace and power from within.

On the journey, we face the essential pain of life and say such things to ourselves as "this takes work" and "I guess I'm not perfect after all." Afterward, we sit in our glow of those elevated emotions, including joy – as well as love, compassion, gratitude, hope, forgiveness, and awe. Then, we get back to work, inspired, energized, and with a renewed zest for life.

Seemingly nothing changes, but truly everything has changed. Soon thereafter, something about that moment of connection and the choice to dig deeper into the predictably gritty emotions and allow life to flow through us delivers. Quite often, miracles, big and small, happen.

Nearly every time I plummet down to a protracted Brain State 5, kicking and screaming all the way, fed up with . . . whatever . . . and stay connected to myself, surrendering to the concept that within me is something good, it passes. Then the next day, something comes from out of nowhere and gives me far more than I had ever hoped for.

You might think of it as the product of neural integration, which is the Lexus of brain configurations, or that the emotional brain is the seat of the soul. Maybe it's the forces of the greater good or a personal connection with the spiritual. However, after facilitating thousands of groups, I know that there is grace in these emotional tools. This magical experience is so common that although the method is scientific, participants often say, "After the 5 comes the 1."

As you take doses of EBT, watch for these moments, but when they occur, strongly consider not sharing the details with others. Words are neocortical, so if you try to explain them, you run the risk of trivializing the multiple layers of emotional experience you have from this method. Besides, these moments are meant for you and you alone, perhaps a sign that you are part of a greater purpose, you do matter, and that there really is something in life . . . whatever that might be . . . that is beyond words.

How do we sustain our immunity? We use times like these to get emotionally honest with ourselves. Most of us do not acknowledge how stressed we are. Instead, we cover over our stress with medications, excesses, and distractions. Our population is extremely stressed, and just saying that can have a calming effect. We can open our minds to the idea that we are far more emotionally powerful than we knew. We can do something about it. We need to own that power and use it.

We can stop being so quick to run to the doctor or therapist to "fix" what is wrong with us. Most problems are caused by the "tail end" of a reactive wire – our response to stress – a behavior, mood, thought, or state that becomes familiar to the brain. Our central nervous system misinterprets it as safe and rewarding until we apply corrective action and deactivate it, and over time, rewire it. If we focus too much on the symptom, we may forget that its root cause is the stress that comes from not knowing how to process the stressed-out emotions that are woven into normal daily life. Instead, we address that root cause, upgrade our emotional processing, and notice that our health begins to improve.

That shift to focusing on how to make stress flow through us is timely. We have never been so polarized and locked into our extreme ways of thinking. This is a symptom of stress. Do not blame people. Blame stress. Everyone is understanding, conciliatory, and compassionate at Brain State 1, and nobody is at Brain State 5.

The more the national and global set points decrease, the more polarized, combative, and short-sighted we become. The sooner we recognize that we have a shared wound – toxic stress – the sooner we will strive to find win-win solutions and have the energy and wisdom to tackle and solve the real problems that face us.

In the past, we have looked to institutions to save us, but they are comprised of stressed-out people. Where do we place our trust? Our only security is inside. We can trust ourselves as, no matter what is happening in the world, we can take a few doses of the stress vaccine and access the magic of the emotional brain. In a state of connection, we are nourished and supported by the seven rewards of a purposeful life.

You can access all of these rewards each time you experience a moment at One – just a flash of them! As you use the method over time, circuits that deliver each of them can become dominant in your brain. You will begin to have confidence that even when Brain State 5 moments come your way, the deep neural pathways of purpose will rise up and remind you of your purpose and reassure you that you do exist, you are not bad, you do have power, you can do good, you can love, you are worthy, and you can have joy.

These enduring messages of emotional security become encoded in the emotional architecture of your brain. You can do that! You can create that safety from within and build an amazing brain by using these emotional techniques. Minecraft is now the most popular videogame of all time. It lets us discover materials, craft tools, and build structures. Yet you have a "mind craft" in your own emotional brain and you can discover circuits, build skills, and create brain structures that are yours and yours alone. It gives you the power to begin to wipe away the past and create a present and future crafted not by your parents, your society, or your personal history, but by who you choose to be, your authentic self.

As you give yourself doses of the stress vaccine, notice that some of the rewards tend to "stick." Their circuits start becoming dominant. Typically, the first reward that becomes dominant is sanctuary. All the other rewards build on the safe base of finding peace and power within. Each of the subsequent rewards strengthens and extends that inner security, eventually radiating that connected state to others. As development continues, the final reward is freedom, being so securely connected to our spiritual core that we have freedom from various attachments and external solutions, and feel complete.

In the EBT method, the longer-term goal is to be "Wired at One," with an abundance of all seven of the richest rewards of life. Our set point is homeostatic, not allostatic. By using this one technique of the method, you will strengthen your resiliency and notice that these higher-order rewards come your way more often. The whole idea of EBT is to start right where you are, enjoy the journey, and see benefits each time you connect with yourself and process your emotions. Your brain will become more emotionally fluid and, like building a muscle, you will build and strengthen your emotional resilience.

What follows are brief descriptions of each reward and a story about someone who made a little magic in their life and the life of the person listening (me) by accessing it.

Reward #1
Sanctuary

Essential Pain: I am alone.
Earned Reward: Peace & power from within

The first reward is sanctuary, feeling peace and power from within. The activation of a reactive wire causes the thinking brain and emotional brain to disconnect. The brain relinquishes control to the reflexive responses of the unconscious mind, the reactive wires.

Instead of soothing, comforting, or rewarding ourselves in healthy ways, we are vulnerable to connecting with a wide range of unhealthy substitutes. We encode a wire that delivers a survival drive to repeat that pattern.

The stress of disconnection can be so overpowering that we have a freeze response and believe that we do not exist. As our stress release changes our physiology, we recognize that we do exist, which poses new challenges. For us to experience existing and being real, like the velveteen rabbit in the children's story, we must face the essential pain that we are alone. No matter how much love we have in our life, we are born alone, die alone, and must take sole responsibility for our choices. That's awakening as we turn our attention to cultivating a sanctuary within to experience peace and power from inside.

Brook had established a comfortable life for her two children, by this time a year after her divorce from Derrick, their father. She had powered through the breakup, having found tell-tale receipts from Derrick's affair with a co-worker in the pockets of his clothes. She had made lists, outsmarted obstacles, and relocated, moving with the children, Ben and Amy, to a smaller place in the same community.

When the stress of the Covid crisis hit, she was dizzy from all the decisions she had to make about her business and the children's schools. Brook's shop, which sold gifts and high-end sundries, had plywood on the windows, and would be unlikely to ever open again. Who bought those inessential things anymore?

All this stress had ignited the unhealed emotional wounds from her divorce, and Brook was feeling overwhelmed. She confided in her business partner that all she could think about was locking herself in her bedroom, curling up in bed with stacks of magazines, drinking rum and orange juice, streaming movies, and never coming out.

Her partner suggested using EBT.

When Brook called for her coaching session, I suggested she launch into using the tools. I knew that if she clarified what was bothering her and expressed her strong negative emotions, positive emotions would follow.

"The situation is . . . my life is a mess. I had everything the way I wanted it, schools for my children, my store, a stable life, and then Derick ruined everything. I stood by my children, and now I have no life. What do I have to look forward to? What I am most stressed about is . . . Covid ruined my life."

Then she paused.

"Does that ring true?"

"No. What I am most stressed about is . . . Derrick ruined my life."

"Well done. Now protest what is happening to you. Give it a burst of red-hot anger. Expletives could help you out here . . ."

"I feel angry that . . . he betrayed me. I can't stand it that . . . he deserted me. I HATE it that . . . everyone in our social circle knew he was screwing that woman, except me. I HATE that he humiliated me. I HATE it that he did that to me. I HATE it that he destroyed my life. I am furious that . . . he didn't love me . . . which makes me sad. I feel sad that . . . I thought he loved me, but he didn't . . ."

"Brook, keep feeling your sadness until it fades . . . then go right into saying 'I feel afraid that . . .'"

"It faded . . . I feel afraid that . . ."

"Find the deepest fear so that you can release the most stress."

"I feel afraid that . . . What I'm most afraid of is . . . I may never recover from this. I may be lonely and unhappy for the rest of my life."

"Take a deep breath and allow your feelings to flow through your body. Extract every bit of healing from them that you can."

Brook took long, deep breaths. Her prefrontal cortex, her emotional brain, and her body took in the feeling, amplified it, then let it go.

"When you are ready, connect with your body and appreciate that you have some power here. In the best of all worlds, what would you have done differently? I feel guilty that . . ."

"I feel guilty that . . . I trusted him. No, that's not right. I feel guilty that . . . I trusted him too much and assumed he loved me as much as I loved him. I gave myself away to him."

Now she was quiet. Her emotional brain was radiating such strong emotions that I felt her sadness in my chest and upper arms.

"Stay in that feeling now. I know this is hard but if you connect a bit more deeply inside . . . your emotional brain will shift from negative emotions to positive ones."

"I can feel it. Something changed. I can feel it in my stomach . . . I feel grateful that . . . I woke up."

She paused again.

"I feel happy that . . . I don't feel happy."

"Of course you don't feel happy, but if you pause for a moment, your emotional brain will bubble up a slight bit of happiness. Take a deep breath. Say the lead-in again."

"I feel a little happy that . . . I have this Covid time to heal."

Brook was joining millions of other Americans in detoxing from the nation's most common socially-acceptable addiction, staying busy-busy-busy, short-changing her brain the unstructured time it needed to process emotions, and ultimately, to update its emotional architecture.

"Wait . . . I have more happiness . . . I feel happy that . . . oh, that's strange . . . I feel happy that . . . I'm not married to that selfish, arrogant man anymore. I feel secure that . . . this will pass at some point. I feel proud that . . . I'm discovering who I am . . ."

"You feel more grounded."

"Yes. I usually merge with other people, I ground myself in their feelings and needs. It's as if I don't even exist. It's all about them!"

Brook paused.

I said, "Connect with yourself and feel a slight glow. When you're ready, let's encode a circuit that enables you to take action with purpose."

"I'm ready."

"I expect myself to do the best I can to . . ."

"I expect myself to do the best I can to . . . I have no idea how to complete that statement. This is sickening. I have either had no expectations or I've borrowed Derrick's. I am a strong woman. Laurel, why would I do that?"

"These wires are encoded in the first few years of life. They are usually intergenerational."

"This must be my mother's wire."

"Perhaps. Others close to us download them into our brains without knowing it. Yet only we can rewire them."

"I'm lost. What's the lead-in?"

"I expect myself to . . ."

"I've got it. I expect myself to do the best I can to . . . ground myself in my body and listen to my own inner voice."

"Does that ring true?"

"Yes, it does."

"Nicely done . . ."

Brook said, "My positive, powerful thought . . . I can learn to do that."

"The essential pain, that hard part for you in following through with grounding yourself in your body and listening to your inner voice?"

"I can't blame other people for my problems. No . . . it's not that . . . it's that I am alone. I have to face the abyss and move through it."

We were both silent, as accepting that essential pain of life is a new beginning. Now Brook had hope. By turning that corner, even if the experience is momentary, she strengthens her resilient wires – her stress antibodies – and weakens the whole range of external solutions she had developed in order to protect herself from facing that essential pain of life.

Facing that changes her. She had a fresh start and like any emotional awakening, not talking, and instead being present to the effervescence of the emotion, is what rewires the deepest circuits in her brain.

"The earned reward of accepting that . . . and following through . . . is that I have myself. It's sanctuary, peace and power from within."

Again, we both paused. A tightness in my chest eased.

"How do you feel now?"

Brook said, "Strange. I am in awe."

"Be gentle with yourself today, and enjoy the subtle excitement and the glow."

"Is that all I have to do?"

"Yes."

"I can do that . . ."

"When you are ready for more, let me know, but you've done enough heavy emotional lifting for today."

Then I gave her a connecting message, kind words that give back to the person who has used the tools, enhancing the emotional experience of the connection.

"Brook, when you did your work, the feelings and sensations in my body were . . . sadness, as it activated some of my memories of divorce, and happiness when you said that Covid would give you time to heal. The way your work was a gift to me was to inspire me to give myself a few more doses to heal those hurts. Thank you."

She thanked me.

"How do you feel now?"

"I feel great. I'm at One."

"What did you learn from your work today?"

"That I don't have to live in the past. Actually, what I'm noticing is some music. It's Paul McCartney singing, 'I'll follow the sun.' That's what I'm going to do. My ex-husband rained on me, but I'm going to follow the sun."

I smiled, "What a great idea. Why not follow the sun?"

Brook said, "I think I'll sing that song to Amy and Ben and start cleaning out my closets. It's time for a change . . ."

The magic of that moment stayed with me and I can imagine it stayed with her. Emotions are like that.

Reward #2
Authenticity
Essential Pain: I am not perfect.
Earned Reward: Feeling whole & being genuine

The second reward is authenticity, feeling whole and being genuine. The triggering of a reactive wire causes extremes, including black and white thinking and the failure to integrate disparate ideas and emotions. We cannot find the shades of gray that are at the core of our more evolved responses.

That same splitting applies to our self-concept. We are all good or all bad, finding it difficult to honor the good in ourselves or humbly appreciate our imperfections. We are not whole and authentic. The second reward is to integrate our light and dark sides and learn to value something more than perfection, the reward of feeling whole and being authentic. We strive to be the best we can be, while lovingly accepting our vulnerabilities. We are not bad, and the essential pain we must accept is that we are not perfect. The flow of emotional rewards from recognizing that keeps us securely grounded in reality and ushers us up to Brain State 1.

Matt's life was disrupted at age 18 by the loss of his mother in an automobile accident. Nobody in the family had the capacity to comfort him or each other. Matt quit school and joined the army, which led him to deployment and combat, from which he had not recovered. His father had moved to Florida. Matt now lived in his family home where he was raised, and he was back working at the local sporting goods store as he had in high school. It was when the coronavirus pandemic caused the store to shut down and Matt to be furloughed that another veteran told him about EBT.

Matt decided to try it and signed up for a coaching session to get started.

When he phoned in, I asked him, "How can I help?"

He said, "I'm not sure. I have buddies I talk with, but I bounce back and forth from being numb to having no control over my temper. I've given up and just try to get through the day. In high school I was a track star and played basketball, so the job at the sporting goods store was my anchor, but I don't think they will open again and if they do, I'm not sure I'd go back."

"On a five-point scale, what is your brain's set point?"

I told him about the numbering system and that the brain had an always-changing state but also a habit or set point, with 5 being the most stressed and 1 being the least stressed.

"That would be 5."

"It's normal at Brain State 5 to not feel rewarded. You might feel like you don't exist, you are bad, or you have no power."

"All of those."

"I want you to be curious."

"Laurel, I am not a curious person. I stopped being curious when that jerk killed my mother when I was 18."

"I want you to not be curious."

"That sounds better."

"Do you want to learn a stress tool?"

"Yes, that's why I am here."

"Are you willing to complain?"

"That's my specialty."

"I will give you the lead-ins. The first two are your complaints. Start with, 'The situation is . . .'"

Matt said, "The situation is . . . I'm a bad person. I don't do anything. I have a son who lives with his mother. He is five years old and she won't let me around him because I can be hot-tempered. Half the time when I call her, she hangs up on me. I don't know when Covid will end and I am not sure I care. One day runs into the next. I talk to several of my buddies in a vet group, but in the last four months, two of them disappeared and our group is dwindling."

"Do you feel done with that one?"

"Yes."

"Now, the next lead-in is: 'What I am most stressed about is . . .' See if your brain will zero in on the one thing that bothers you the most. If you can release stress from that one thing, you will begin to feel somewhat better."

"What I am most stressed about is . . . my ex-wife won't let me see my son."

"Nicely done. Pause until you feel connected to your body."

He laughed and said, "I never feel connected to my body."

"That's fine. You can skip that part if you like."

"No, I'll try. Give me a minute."

A few minutes went by.

Matt said, "I feel more connected."

All of us have stuck emotions at times. The challenge is to unpack them in keeping with the stress vaccine. Without that skill to turn stuck emotions into flowing feelings, the reptilian brain, with chronic stress and reactivity, changes the course of our lives. The essential first step in this unpacking is expressing anger, which is then soothed, calmed, and therefore made safe by expressing the feelings that follow it in the technique: sadness, fear, and guilt. For Matt, experiencing that natural flow of emotions could give him instant improvement in his experience of toxic anger.

"The next step is to express your anger. Use the lead-ins of I feel angry that . . . I can't stand it that . . . and I HATE it that, then keep going for up to one minute. After that, we'll move into sadness, which will blunt the anger and keep it safe."

"I feel angry that . . . my mind just went blank . . . I can't stand it that . . . still not feeling anything. I feel . . . FUCKING angry that I have nothing good in my life. I HATE it that my mother died. I HATE it that I cannot see my son. I HATE it that his mother treats me like an animal. I HATE it that I have no power and I really hate it that she judges me. Who the FUCK is she to judge me? I hate that and I hate her!"

With that, Matt burst out sobbing.

He cried for a minute or two.

"Stay with your feelings until you can find your deepest sadness, just one sadness, as that helps you feel the feelings and activates healing . . ."

"I feel sad that . . . she judges me."

"Now feel your sadness for as long as you can. Do not use words. Just feel it flow through your body."

He was silent.

"It flowed slightly, but now I don't feel sad anymore."

"You have done this really well. You're almost there. Now make one statement for each emotion."

"Okay . . . I feel afraid that . . . I will never see my son again. I feel guilty that . . . I screwed up so much . . . I feel grateful that . . . I don't feel grateful."

"You can quit now if you want or give that feeling another try. Say, 'I feel a little grateful that . . .'"

"I feel a little grateful that . . . I have a few buddies."

"I feel happy that . . . I have a son. I feel secure that . . . I love my son . . . and I feel FUCKING proud that I'm getting help for this."

"Matt, that was beautiful. Now you need inner stability, a plan to go forward. The lead-in is, 'I expect myself to do the best I can to . . .'"

"I expect myself to do the best I can to . . . own up to my problem with anger and do something about it."

"Excellent. Now say some encouraging words."

"My positive, powerful thought . . . This is the right time to do this."

"What is the hard part you would have to face to follow through?"

"My essential pain is . . . I am not perfect."

"That's right. The stress from your mother's death, the combat, and more tells you that you have to be perfect or you are a bad person. When the brain in stress releases those messages, the stress hormone cortisol, which is public health enemy #1, or maybe now #2 after Covid, diminishes the brain's capacity to hold two opposite realities and integrate them. If we cannot be perfect, then we must be bad."

"It's more like I am the worst person who ever walked the face of this earth."

"Say it again and feel that in your body until it fades."

Matt was quiet.

"Shit, who is perfect anyway? I am not perfect, and I don't have to be."

"Sounds good. Stay with the feeling as long as you can until you have extracted every bit of healing you can from it. Get your money's worth out of it."

Humor helps the method.

"Okay, it faded . . . and my reward is . . . authenticity, feeling whole and being genuine."

I asked, "How do you feel now?"

He said, "Like a ton of bricks is off my chest. I didn't know I could feel anger without going into a rage."

I gave him a connecting message, a way that peers or providers can give back emotionally in a safe way after someone has taken their dose.

"Matt, when you did your work, the feelings and sensations in my body were . . . sadness, and then I noticed my cheeks tense up a bit, and then a slight smile. The way your work was a gift to me in my own use of the tools was . . . I liked the way you used expletives even when you were expressing positive emotions. I might try that. Thanks."

"I'm glad I could help you out."

I smiled and told him, "Take one dose per day."

Matt's set point was in stress overload. Keeping his

dose very low at first would make it easier for his brain to accept a new way of processing stress.

"Why not more?"

"Your reptilian brain will not like changing how you process stress. A slow introduction to the tools is less likely to make the reptile snappish."

"What happened? Why didn't I do what I usually do and go into a rage?"

"It's a vaccine."

"Don't bullshit me."

"Look at it this way, when your mom died, it was so traumatic that your emotions became toxic."

"That's true."

"To heal that hurt, you have to feel the feelings you suppressed at that time."

"I went numb, and I drank or broke things."

"It's a 'vaccine' of sorts, as once you learn how to process toxic emotions, you have that skill for life."

"Where were you 20 years ago when I needed you?"

I felt a stab of sadness and said, "I'm sorry I wasn't here."

He paused, caught off guard by my sorrow, and said, "Well, you're here now."

"Matt, you can heal by processing your emotions day by day, and I'll help you."

"I'd like that."

The power of using the tools with loving connection was opening him up.

"Great, I'll see you next week."

Matt said, "Yes, you will!"

Reward #3
Vibrancy

Essential Pain: I am not in complete control.
Earned Reward: Healthy with a zest for life

The third reward is vibrancy, healthy with a zest for life. A reactive wire disconnects us from awareness of the sensations and emotions in our body. We lose the grounding effect of feedback from our body, and optimal health stays just beyond our reach. We lose our power.

As our emotional clearing reveals an experience that, in fact, we do have power, we must confront another reality of life. We are not in complete control. If we can face that, our whole body relaxes. We are not in complete control – what a relief! We do have power and we use it without venturing into overcontrol. We are healthy with a zest for life!

Christine was one of those people who laugh for no reason. You're not sure why she is laughing, but you know it's earnest and you want more of what she has. She had a middle-class upbringing and was drawn to social justice and helping the underserved. She liked giving so much to others but the added stress of Covid was beginning to take its toll on her.

She called into our session and said, "I'm working with the homeless now. I help them get connected with social services, make medical appointments for them, give them fresh clothes, and sometimes bring homemade cookies. The risk of Covid is high."

I asked, "How can I help?"

"I'm exhausted, and my husband is having hip surgery. I don't have children, but I have a large community of people who depend on me for emotional support. I'm drained."

"Let's use the lead-ins of the technique and see what your emotional brain has to say about it."

Christine began, "The situation is . . . during the day I am with people who have been abused, neglected, and forgotten by society. I talk to them, and take oral histories that they can keep, so I know their pain. Now my husband needs my help with his surgery and I'm exhausted and I don't know my limits – physically because of Covid, and emotionally. I'm bordering on burnout."

"What are you most stressed about?"

"What I am most stressed about is . . . I only have so much energy. I only have so much time. I'm 70 years old and I am feeling it and don't know what to do."

"Again, what are you are most stressed about?"

"I am running out of energy."

"Can you protest that with anger?"

"I feel angry that . . . I am running out of energy. I can't stand it that . . . life is not forever . . . I HATE it that . . . I am vulnerable to the virus. I feel angry that . . . I am sad more than angry. I feel sad that . . . I won't always be here. I feel afraid that . . . I will run out of energy before I run out of love. I feel guilty that . . . I never really thought I would run out. I thought I would live forever . . . and my time and energy would not fade."

I took a deep breath, as someone who is older myself, I understood.

116

Christine said, "I feel grateful that . . . I am still trying to give back. I feel happy that . . . I can help my husband when he needs it. I feel secure that . . . I am helping people. I feel proud that . . . I am noticing that I have limitations."

"What about your actions?"

"I expect myself to do the best I can to . . . use my power to shine and help people for as long as I can . . . My positive, powerful thought . . . That is the right thing to do. The essential pain is . . . I am not in complete control. I do not know how long my energy will last. My earned reward is . . . vibrancy. As long as I can move forward, I'm going to do it being healthy with a zest for life."

"How do you feel now?"

"A little joyful and a little sad."

"I understand. If you are grounded in your body and moving forward with purpose, all the positive emotions have an underbelly of loss. They imbed the realities of life, which means that we have a natural high but not an addictive one."

Christine said, "That helps me. I am going to go forward, and I appreciate that I am not in complete control. I'm going to give myself doses of the stress vaccine and process my emotions. I will be of service as long as I can while staying healthy with a zest for life."

"How do you feel now?"

"Happier. I will take care of my husband and myself and be healthy with a zest for life as long as I possibly can."

"What did you learn from your work today?"

"How fulfilled I am. How grateful I am to work with the homeless. And a sobering message, that I value my vibrancy, and I will protect it. I want a zest for life. That matters to me."

The human desire to help others is so strong that it is easy to lose our boundaries and give more than we have to give. On a neuronal level, that willingness to open up our hearts to others means allowing their toxic stress wires to enter our emotional brain so that we can feel their feelings. Healing follows. However, there is a price to pay: their circuits can rattle around in our unconscious mind for hours or days.

Instead, Christine was developing a brain-based health approach to her work, celebrating and expressing her strong socially-unacceptable emotions without self-judgment. By using the lead-ins, she could express rip-roaring anger – whether it was toward the government, the homeless, the spiritual, or life itself – and bounce back to One. She was learning to reject the tyranny of constant compassion, which is rampant these days in favor of emotional honesty.

That single practice could allow her to experience the joy of giving for years to come.

Reward #4
Integrity
Essential Pain: It takes work.
Earned Reward: Doing the right thing

The fourth reward is integrity, doing the right thing. As we draw upon our energies to use our talents in just the ways that make us feel complete (and survive), we must be industrious and charge forward, experiencing many failures, some victories, and sometimes persevering long after it stops being edifying or fun.

A reactive wire wipes away our self-confidence and fills us with self-doubt, but as we have an emotional clearing, we return to a reasonable expectation. We can do good. That's encouraging until we realize that to do good, it takes work, a lot of work. Facing that essential pain that life will require more of us than, at times, we believe we can muster, enables us to smile, relax, and follow through. We accomplish things that are hard and are guided by our gut feel of what is the right thing to do. We have that moral compass and chemical surges of self-respect follow.

Stella had lost her husband to cancer in late 2019, and she had a history of depression. Exercise was her way of coping, and she had made plans with her best friend from college to walk part of the Pacific Coast Trail in June 2020.

Then, in April, a nurse at the skilled nursing facility her father was in was so exhausted from pandemic stress that she dropped him, and he broke his femur. In the hospital, he contracted an antibiotic-resistant staph infection and passed away. A week later, exhausted, Stella tripped over her dad's dog's leash, fell hard onto the concrete in her backyard, fracturing her knee, and she was stuck on the ground for two hours before her next-door neighbor Jessica heard her cries and called an ambulance.

Stella was already taking antidepressants. Her therapist recommended EBT as a "bolt-on" to therapy to support her progress.

She said during our first coaching session, "I don't want to talk to anybody, even my neighbor Jessica who rescued me. My mind is frozen with stress. My dad's dog comes up to me and whines for attention and I have no interest. I want help in using the tools."

Stella was so stressed that she needed to take several doses of EBT. This is a "dig deeper" use of the tools that clears away emotional stress in layers.

"Start where you are. You may need to give yourself several doses in a row. That helps your brain loosen up toxic emotions and encourages them to flow."

"My brain feels stuck, like there is no way this will ever change."

"That's what the lizard brain does to us. It convinces us that we will never dig out of this, that we are a burden to everyone, and that there is no hope. You'll win over the inner reptile, you'll see."

Stella said, "What took me over the edge is that I can't go on the Pacific Crest Trail hike because of the pandemic and my knee injury. I have nothing to look forward to . . . all I feel is doom and gloom."

"Let's do something about that . . . Just begin."

"The situation is . . . I can't have anything I want. My husband is gone, my father is gone, my knee will take a year to heal, I'm in bloody pain, and I can't go on my hike. I don't know what I did to deserve this . . . and I listen to my own harsh inner voice and the horrible things I say to myself and then my mind goes numb. I think my brain is a lump of coal."

"What I am most stressed about is . . ."

"What I am most stressed about is . . . I don't have anything to look forward to . . ."

"I feel angry that . . ."

"I feel angry that . . . I have no anger."

She needed to wind her way out of the depression ditch and after the session, I would double-check her plan for support with her therapist and physician, but the underlying cause of her depression was having a greater stress load coming into her brain than she had the emotional tools to process. She could treat that with the stress vaccine.

"Of course you cannot feel anger because you're in the depression ditch, but let's be creative here and change the lead-in to 'I feel *slightly* angry that . . .'"

Stella said, "I feel slightly angry that . . . nobody cares about me. I feel slightly angry that . . . I don't care about myself . . . I can't stand it that . . . my dad is dead. I really hate it that . . . I don't really hate it . . . That's all the anger I've got."

"That's perfect. You're being authentic and using the power of unconditional love of yourself. Right now, your beautiful emotional brain is stuck and you have no more anger."

121

"That's right."

"Great. Let's use just one deep sadness to keep it tender rather than letting sadness go into depression."

"I feel sad that . . . what I'm most sad about is . . . I have nothing to look forward to."

"I know that's hard to say, but your voice was tender. Wonderful. Feel the sadness in your body until it fades and turns to fear."

"I am already at fear. I feel afraid that . . . I will never feel better. The same thing that happened to my dad will happen to me. I will never survive this . . ."

"Stay in your feelings, then notice that the fear fades."

"It's fading . . . I feel guilty that . . . my part of this is . . . I don't know."

"Try saying, 'I do have some power here. Why don't I just . . .'"

Stella said, "I do have some power here . . . why don't I just . . . get over it?"

The guilt statement is very important, as it identifies what we could do differently, not what we "should" do if we were perfect, but the sensible action to take that would improve our situation. Just stating that activates the wires that cause us to be stuck, and pausing to feel our feelings at that time begins to passively rewire them.

"Stay with your feelings, then move to 'I feel a little grateful that . . .' when you are ready."

"I feel a little grateful that . . . I am alive . . . I feel a little happy that . . . I have a bed to sleep in . . . I feel secure that . . . it's not my fault. I feel proud that . . . I am opening up about my feelings."

"I expect myself . . ."

"I expect myself to do the best I can to . . . not judge myself for my feelings. I expect myself to . . . be as depressed as I need to be for as long as I need to be."

Although her expectation may sound negative, what's important is that it rings true. If it rings true to her, then she is using her prefrontal cortex to lovingly observe herself and that secure, warm connection will switch off legions of reactive circuits if it is accomplished just after she has unlocked the wire with the stress of healthy anger.

"My positive, powerful thought . . . I have the power to do that . . . The essential pain is . . . I am not in complete control . . . and my earned reward is . . . authenticity."

"How do you feel now?"

Stella said, "2-ish."

"Do you want to take another dose?"

"I might as well. I want to rediscover the happy person I was . . ."

She paused before continuing.

"I have this image of myself when my husband and I hiked in the Tetons in Wyoming the year we were married. I can see the green meadows and the purple mountains and smell the fresh air. I want to feel that way again . . ."

"You can have that."

"How many doses does it take?"

"You never know. Each one counts, but these are emotional circuits, of all sizes and strengths. We never know if the next dose will transform it and something magical will occur. Each cycle through your emotions is unique, and you are the first to know how it worked. You can feel it!"

"Let's dig deeper. The situation is . . . I want to hide. I don't want to see anyone, and I know that is not healthy, but I don't care. What I am most stressed about is . . . I don't want to be a burden to people . . ."

At this point, she was in the flow of the universal process of humanity, which is to process our emotions. It's allowing whatever stress had accumulated within her to move through her body – whoosh! – and coming out the other side feeling more peace and power from within.

I guided Stella through two more doses of the technique, until she had released the Brain State 5, and was spiraling up to a Brain State 1. That's the special magic of the radical resiliency experience of "after the 5 comes the 1."

"I expect myself to do the best I can to . . ."

Stella paused and seemed to connect even more deeply with herself.

"I expect myself to do the best I can to . . . deal with my reality."

She gasped.

"That's what I want. This is my reality. My father died. My husband died. I injured my knee. I can't do what I love, which is hiking, but I want to learn how to deal with that."

Her voice was full of energy with a tinge of joy.

"My positive, powerful thought . . . it's time. I can do that . . . The essential pain is . . . it takes work. My earned reward is . . . integrity."

"Integrity?"

"That's right. Integrity, doing the right thing. I don't have to wallow in my grief anymore. People all over the planet are in toxic stress. People are sick and dying, losing their jobs and their homes. I am going to embrace my reality and feel grateful for all that I have. I know that the loss and pain I have had mark a new beginning for me. I don't know what the future holds, but I do know that I am in love with myself and in love with my life, no matter what."

I smiled and said, "After the 5 comes the 1."

She was in a glow state and we both sat with that for a few moments. How did she get from Brain State 5 to Brain State 1, both of which are extreme states? These are the only two reward states, as endorphins flow at Brain State 5 in anticipation of physical injury, a throwback to our hunter-gatherer ancestors, and at Brain State 1, too, which could be a factor. The research is not clear. However, in Brain State 5, oxytocin, the love chemical, is high. One explanation for this unexpectedly high oxytocin level at Brain State 5 may be that evolutionary biology favored a chemical release that supported reaching out and connecting with people or going inside and connecting with the spiritual in times of stress overload. That connection is what catapults us to One.

I gave her a connecting message.

"Stella, when you did your work, the feelings and sensations in my body were . . . profound sadness that you are going through this. The way your work was a gift to me was . . . I remembered when my mother passed away, I went outside onto the lawn behind my house and threw my body down on the grass like people do when they make snow angels. I surrendered to my feelings and that changed the course of my grieving. Thank you for bringing up that special memory for me."

"Thank you, Laurel."

"How do you feel now?"

"I'm at One."

"What did you learn from your work today?"

"I learned that there is love inside me. I just need to be persistent and dig deeper – take more doses – and I can find it."

Stella would be likely to remember that dose even decades later. The brain strongly remembers the occasions when we radically switch our emotional states, perhaps as a way of bringing us hope.

We are born with an emotional brain that enables us to be present to enough pain to motivate us to keep digging inside. The deeper we go emotionally, the more we find what is at our very core: love.

Reward #5
Intimacy

Essential Pain: Some people may reject me.
Earned Reward: Giving & receiving love

The fifth reward is intimacy, giving and receiving love. A toxic stress wire makes it virtually impossible for us to find love inside and believe that we can love. Are we loveable? Probably not. Can we connect to the love that is waiting in the wings within us? That's hard to imagine when cortisol, with all its fight-or-flight judgments, is surging.

As we release stress, our unconscious mind begins to believe that we can love. Maybe it is worth a try. However, just as we regain our confidence and resolve, an essential pain of life becomes evident. Some people may reject us. Even though that hurts, as we are fortified with the unconscious emotional message that even if they do, we will not reject ourselves, we move forward. We have the courage to give and receive love, within the limits of our circumstances, the joy of intimacy.

Helene was not a pushover. She was a psychiatrist, compassionate, but very opinionated and demanding. She had married Raymond because they were so much alike. He was a trial lawyer and their lively intellectual conversations kept them happily enthralled with one another.

Then came Covid, and their reactive circuits were suddenly firing emotional bombs at one another. Their marriage became as polarized politically as the country. They couldn't see each other's point of view and each was incensed that the other was so utterly deluded.

Helene had been part of the EBT community for about a year and had a weekly group and many connection buddies for support. However, her fury at Raymond had reached new extremes as the pandemic stress whittled away at her patience and he began drinking more. When Raymond was drinking, she felt like she was being cross-examined and she found him completely obnoxious to the point where she was seriously considering whether they had any chance at all of repairing their relationship.

She started the coaching session, saying, "Laurel, I need to let it rip."

"That's why we're here."

"The situation is . . . I am married to a complete idiot who actually believes that there is a conspiracy worldwide that is faking the pandemic and there is a multinational organization that is playing chess with the world and is out to produce a global depression for their own power and gain. This man is so thick-skulled that my eyes bug out when I even start to talk with him about it and now he's mad at me for my political beliefs, so he is getting back at me by withholding sex. It's been three months since I have had any sexual satisfaction or affection and by now I don't even care. Why would I want to make love with a complete and utter idiot?"

She paused, a sign that she had emptied her emotional brain of what it needed her to express, and she was ready to move to the next lead-in.

"What I am most stressed about is . . . I am married to a pathetic conspiracy theory idiot. I feel ANGRY that . . . he actually believes this shit. I can't stand it that . . . he is that delusional. I can't stand it that he thinks he is RIGHT! Actually, that makes me sad . . ."

Helene's anger skill was exceptional as she was a practiced EBTer, and she knew how to use emotions and carefully selected expletives to their best effect. When her emotions turned to sadness, she had fulfilled her need for A+ Anger so she moved to the next lead-in.

"I feel sad that . . . this is driving us apart . . ."

She wept softly for several minutes.

Then she said, "I feel afraid that . . . Covid will ruin our marriage . . ."

She paused, again extracting every healing force possible from feeling that fear until it faded.

"I feel guilty that . . ."

At that moment, she let out a hoot.

She had experienced a rapid, extreme, and positive change in her state. She had popped. We believe this is caused by the amygdala, or stress center, shutting off and the right prefrontal cortex, associated with positive emotions, becoming activated. This is one of the signs of radical resilience.

"I feel grateful that . . . I love Raymond so much. I feel happy that . . . he is even talking to me. This whole Covid mess has been so hard for both of us. I feel secure that . . . my love for him is more vast and deep than ever. And I feel proud that . . . I can forgive him for being so delusional . . ."

Now she was laughing and crying at the same time.

"I expect myself to do the best I can to . . . love Raymond and let him have whatever crazy opinions he has about politics and then move on to deal with other issues between us. I expect myself to do the best I can to . . . lead with love. My positive, powerful thought? He is not perfect, and neither am I. Essential pain? He may reject me for my views, but even if he does, I won't reject myself. My earned reward? Intimacy, giving and receiving love."

I asked how she felt.

"Happy, loving, loved, and forgiving!"

"What did you learn from your dose?"

"I learned that I love Raymond and I trust that whatever his reasons for his conspiracy theory, this man is all about purpose. It's probably integrity, he believes he is doing the right thing, which is why I have my opinion, too. Integrity. So, we share what is most important."

"What beautiful work, Helene!"

In just a few minutes, she had made a shift in mindset that allowed her stuck emotions to flow. Only after being emotionally honest with ourselves and releasing our stress with strong emotions – the A+ Anger and the natural flow of the feelings that follows – do we find ourselves at Brain State 1. This is the only state of intimacy. Brain State 2 is not an intimate state. It is a functional state only. Brain States 3, 4, and 5 are states in which there is no intimacy, and we treat ourselves and others like objects.

Helene needed to process her emotions, get past the specifics, and be aware of their shared values and rewards. Given how diverse and extreme our population is, conflicting opinions will continue. The quality of love in our relationships and in our nation is dependent upon people having the emotional tools to go beyond thoughts and peer into one another's brain to find shared purpose.

After the 5 comes the 1. Helene happily concluded the session by saying, "Thanks, Laurel. I feel much better."

"What will you do differently now, Helene?"

"I will exhale and focus on what matters most to me right now: loving myself, loving others, and getting through this horrendous time with more love in my life, not less."

I said, "What a wonderful way to live!"

Reward #6
Spirituality
Essential Pain: I must receive.
Earned Reward: Grace, beauty & mystery of life

The sixth reward is spirituality, being aware of the grace, beauty, and mystery of life. As our connections to ourselves and others deepen, we hunger to discover the more profound meanings of life. The most important relationship of all – the connection to the deepest part of ourselves – calls to us. It is haunting at first, but as stress-reactivity fades, that inner connection becomes our passion and power.

The stress-fueled notion that we are not worthy – a product of a reactive wire – fades, and like it or not, we find we are worthy of not only love but of being part of some larger need to give back. Yet that takes recognizing ourselves as wanting and needing a certain selflessness. We are not only of this world but have a need to surrender to something that is beyond ourselves. Instead of becoming all-powerful, we open ourselves to asking for support. We allow the magic of the world, as we define it, to nourish and guide us.

With that surrender often comes an awakening to the natural pleasures of life. We see beauty everywhere. Love abounds where before we never noticed it. We may begin nourishing ourselves with life's bounty, becoming even more capable of being of service to the greater good. We become acutely aware of the grace, beauty, and mystery of life. A spiritual connection, however we define it, lights up our lives.

As a psychology professor for graduate students, Jenny had a gift for teaching, and her passion was mentoring students, then keeping in touch with them over the years. They were her family of choice. She lived with her cat, Beatrice, and started her EBT practice because of her weight.

She said, "When I was writing my dissertation, I disconnected from my body and stopped taking care of myself. I put on 50 pounds, then another 50, and that trend has not stopped."

She had used healthy eating and various diets, but she would always gain the weight back when she was stressed. Stress triggers wires that unleash chemicals, causing cravings, lethargy, depression, and weight gain. The obesity epidemic is caused not just by a glut of sugar in our food supply, but by physiological stress: sugar binges increase metabolic stress, extra weight causes physical stress, and the fat-shaming of our culture activates psychological stress. The obesity epidemic is just another symptom of our nation's failure to eradicate toxic stress.

Jenny said, "The situation is . . . I love my students and I have put up a wall against their judgments about my body, because I know I can win them over in time. Now, they judge me *more* because if I am infected with Covid, and I die, it would be *my* fault, because I have no willpower."

"What I'm most stressed about is . . . I have let their judgment cause me to be filled with self-loathing . . . I hate that!"

"Let it rip, Jenny!"

"I feel furious that I internalize their judgments and turn their 5 states into my own, and then I go to 5 . . . or 10."

"Keep it short and choppy, Jenny, express the activations in your unconscious mind, not in your neocortex."

"I get it. I feel angry that . . . actually, I feel FURIOUS that the enemy is inside. I HATE it that I do it to myself. I can't stand it that I have this huge body that isn't even me. I HATE it that they pity me. I HATE it that they judge me. I HATE IT!!!! I HATE myself. I hate them. I hate this fat. I HATE it all!!!"

She paused.

"Ohhhh, that felt wonderful. I REALLY needed that."

"Wait until you feel connected again, then find your deepest sadness, and feel it until it fades. Get all the benefit from that sadness that you can."

"I feel sad that . . . What I'm most sad about is . . . oh my gosh, that's interesting. What I'm most sad about it that they don't love me."

She breathed deeply several times, allowing that sadness to flow through her body.

"I feel afraid that, what I'm most afraid of is that . . . that's a surprise, too . . . What I'm most afraid of is . . . I will die."

"I feel guilty that . . . I want to quit teaching."

Every feeling she felt – sadness, fear, and guilt – were complete surprises to Jenny. She had mastered the technique enough to get her thinking brain out of the way and peer into her emotional brain with its circuits that define who she is. She was experiencing the joy of a deeper knowledge of herself. Only by knowing ourselves can our unconditional self-love deepen and nourish our spirits.

"Holy shit!" she exclaimed.

I laughed.

Jenny laughed.

"Stay with your negative emotions until the positive ones overpower them. You may feel an effervescence in your body, a slight burning or tingling in some area, perhaps your limbs or abdomen. Stay with it until the positive emotions predominate."

She breathed deeply for a few more seconds, then said, "I got it! I feel grateful that . . . I love myself. I feel happy that . . . I am not buying into their emotions and judgments. I feel secure that . . . under their stress, they do feel love for me. I feel proud that . . . I am rediscovering what a strong warrior of the world I am!"

I was chuckling by this time.

"I expect myself to do the best I can to . . . connect to the love inside of me and inspire my students to love more and learn the theories I'm teaching them!"

Now she was in such a flow that she charged forward rapidly with the remainder of the lead-ins.

"My positive, powerful thought . . . I am perfectly capable of doing that. The essential pain is . . . I must receive. To me, that is surrendering to the love inside me and feeling my connection to the sacred in life."

Again, she paused, then said, "My earned reward is . . . spirituality."

I am guessing we were both tingling from the magic of the moment.

"How do you feel now, Jenny?"

"Excited. Happy. Grateful. Proud."

"What did you learn from your work today?"

She paused for a moment, then said, "I learned that . . . I love myself more than I knew, and I am not giving up teaching. The stress of Covid is bringing out the warrior for the good in me."

The stress of the pandemic activates some of the circuits that make us most vulnerable. If it had not been for the extra layer of shaming and fears Jenny had about her students due to Covid, she might not have discovered these deeper meanings of her life.

The joy of adversity is that it presents us with opportunities to clear away emotional abscesses from the past and to fall in love with the goodness within ourselves, which was just what Jenny had done.

Her loving connection to herself was instantly transmitted to my emotional brain, as the emotional brain has no walls. We both basked for a moment in our reverberating love circuits and enjoyed the magic of two emotional brains in connection.

Over time, as Jenny clears away her stress-reactive circuits and connects even more deeply with herself, food would lose its control over her. She would experience all seven of the rewards of a purposeful life. Her struggles with weight gave her just what she needed, the emotional skills to connect to the deepest part of herself.

What more could anyone need than that?

Reward #7
Freedom

Essential Pain: I must give.
Earned Reward: Common excesses fade

The seventh reward is freedom, when common excesses fade and we soar. We feel complete and experience an expansive love for ourselves, others, and life. A reactive wire doesn't have a chance to send us down, and our brain is all about crashing through the messiness of life, accepting the gifts of it, then creating even more joy in our lives.

A reactive wire tells us that we cannot have joy. Life is that difficult, as although we have accepted so much of the essential pain of life, we are asked to accept even more, and to do it even if our bodies and brains are shopworn and seem far from adequate. As our emotional clarity comes forth, we sense that, to our surprise, we must give at a deeper level. We don't think about it. We just do it and by choosing to give more, the reward of freedom seems to drop out of the heavens. We want that sense of being complete, using our talents to their fullest, and feeling the glow of knowing that, imperfect as we are, we've done the best that we can do and that is enough. Finally, we are free.

Thomas was about to be a father for the first time. He was working in tech and so was his wife, Gretchen. Thomas tried out EBT because he was scared.

He called in and said, "I am the first member of my family to graduate from college, and among the six children in my family, the only one who is not an addict. Gretchen is eight weeks pregnant, she has morning sickness, and I am scared out of my mind that I am going to make a mistake. I don't want to screw up and pass along wires to my kid that I don't even know I have."

"Bring Gretchen to the phone. The biggest gift you can give your child is an emotionally honest relationship between the two of you. Everyone has some reactive circuits, and if you both know how to connect emotionally with yourself, your baby, and each other, that is a physiological home run."

He agreed.

Gretchen joined the call. She said she felt a little ill, bringing back memories of my own pregnancies.

I said, "The most profound gift you can give your baby is for both of you to become emotionally resilient. Only then will you on both conscious and unconscious levels transmit resilient wires to the baby. This is one thing you cannot buy and can only earn by doing the emotional work. There is no hiding – your baby will sense your brain state even before you do."

Thomas asked, "Where do we begin?"

"You begin with the rewards. What reward do you most want for yourself and your baby?"

Thomas said, "With my family history of addiction, freedom."

Gretchen said, "Sanctuary, peace and power from within, and it's important that we give our baby freedom, not just from addiction but from false attachments. I want my child to be wired for joy, to be at One, and to have the brain power to deal with anything that comes their way."

With all of us facing so much fear about the external world and all its conflict, extremes, and uncertainty, how can any parent relax and feel secure that they are giving their child a great start in life?

"If you give your new baby one thing that will make the most difference in their life, it is the power to process stress effectively and feel grounded, then move forward with higher purpose. If they learn the emotional tools of radical resilience, they will create a magnificent life for themselves."

Thomas said, "How can I do that?"

I said, "You are the pathway. You are the solution."

He said, "Now I'm feeling cornered. I want to do everything I can to give our baby the best crib, the best pediatrician, the right vaccines . . . and we're even having a home birth in warm water with a midwife. We're six minutes away from the hospital, so we have that covered if something goes wrong."

I said, "That's the easy stuff. If you want to do this right, then you are the solution, your capacity to lean into strong negative emotions, and not duck out and play videogames or work late at the office. When Gretchen is hormonal and impossible to be with, you need to be at Brain State 1, so you know when to comfort her and when to set some gentle but helpful limits. These are really hard things for the brain to do. It takes emotional courage to do that."

Thomas said, "I need a dose."

I said, "That's great, Thomas! Follow the lead-ins in your app. Gretchen, would you please be a warm presence for Thomas while he processes his emotions? Don't interrupt him. Don't criticize him. Do not bring up the content of his work later on, and be ready to give him a connecting message when he is done."

Gretchen said, "I can do that."

I said, "Thomas, start right where you are . . ."

Thomas said, "The situation is . . . I have no confidence that I can be a father. My father was an alcoholic and my mother was clinically depressed and gambled the family's money away. I have no idea what I am doing."

After a pause, he continued, "What I am most stressed about is . . . I'll be a loser as a dad . . . I feel angry that . . . I don't know what I am doing . . . I feel sad that . . ."

"Good work, Thomas, but you've been through a lot and there is a lot of opportunity here. You could use your own brain to download into your baby the resiliency pathways that will prevent so much of the suffering your family went through. The stronger your emotions, the deeper in the brain they go to rewire your brain for radical resilience."

He said, "I don't know how to be emotionally honest. I never learned that."

"You complain."

"I don't do that."

"Are you willing to give it a try and see how clean it feels?"

He said, "Okay."

"Start over. It doesn't matter what you process, but it matters that you process something that actually upsets you."

Thomas said, "I'll try that . . . The situation is . . . Gretchen is eight weeks pregnant and she is still drinking a glass of wine every night . . ."

Gretchen jumped in, "Who are *you* to say that? *You're using weed and that's just what your two brothers did before they switched to painkillers and tequila. Who are you to blame me?*"

I said, "This is really challenging. Gretchen, what kind of circuit are you running?"

She said, "I don't care!"

I paused.

She said, "I'm reactive. I'm at 5 and I'm toxic!"

I said, "Fantastic! When you said that, my whole body relaxed."

She said, "Why?"

"You were authentic and vulnerable."

She let out a small gasp.

"You don't have to listen to Thomas process his emotions. Just tell him you're stressed and need to take a break for a few minutes, but you will be back. Or, you can listen without interrupting him."

Gretchen said, "I am too stressed to listen to him. I need to use the technique."

I said, "Both of you are stressed, and it doesn't matter to me who uses the technique first. Thomas, what is your preference?"

He said, "Gretchen can go first. That's fine with me."

"Great. Gretchen, whenever you are ready, please begin . . ."

"Thanks, Thomas . . . The situation is . . . my husband is talking about me having a glass of wine. I'm the one who is pregnant and being so careful about almost everything, and he is completely detached, smoking weed,

141

playing videogames, and totally disconnected from me. What I'm most stressed about is . . . I feel so lonely."

"You did that well. That is your topic: you feel lonely. Now protest the fact that you feel lonely. Express some healthy anger . . ."

"I feel angry that . . . he plays videogames, smokes weed, and doesn't care about me."

"That was effective anger, but if you can, stay with the topic, as you'll release more stress that way. Keep your anger about being alone. Your emotional brain will do the elegant work of activating and updating the wires that cause you to feel stressed."

Gretchen expressed her fury, "I feel ANGRY that . . . I feel so lonely. I CAN'T STAND it that . . . I am so very, very lonely. I HATE it that I'm married and am pregnant but still feel so ALONE! I HATE THAT!!! I really HATE THAT!!!"

She was clearing away months or years of suppressed emotions.

I encouraged her, "Stay in anger until it becomes sadness, Gretchen."

"It's already sadness. I feel sad that . . . I am so lonely . . . I feel afraid that I will never be happy even though I am having a baby. I feel guilty that . . . I stuff my feelings, then when I can't take it anymore, I start screaming at Thomas or drinking wine . . ."

"Very well done, but try the I feel guilty lead-in again to identify the one thing that in the best of all worlds you wish you would do."

"In the best of all worlds, I wish that . . . I wouldn't scream at my husband."

She was quiet.

"Beautifully done! If you can, stay aware of your body and feel your feelings until they fade. Feeling your feelings now, after you have stress-activated them, is what rewires these old reactive wires."

She paused, then said, "I feel lighter. The stress is going away."

"Wonderful . . . now, the positive emotions."

"I feel grateful that . . . this is out in the open. I feel happy that . . . we are talking about it. I feel secure that . . . I will not be lonely for the rest of my life! I feel proud that . . . even though I am not perfect, and Thomas is not perfect, I know he loves me, and I know I love him."

Gretchen had done it! She was at One. She had used her radical resilience pathway.

I said, "Now, savor this moment . . ."

"I can feel the glow, but I want to go on . . . I expect myself to do the best I can to . . . process my emotions and get to One, so I feel connected to myself."

"Beautiful! Now, what is your positive, powerful thought?"

"I must do this. My baby is important. I am important. Our marriage is important!"

"The essential pain . . ."

"The essential pain is . . . I am not perfect. My earned reward is . . . authenticity, feeling whole and being genuine."

"Do you feel a surge of joy?"

She said, "YES!!!"

I said, "Thomas, would you like to give Gretchen a connecting message?"

He said, "Yes, Gretchen, when you did your work, the feelings and sensations in my body were . . . sadness. I don't like you being lonely. And guilt . . . that I have been so obsessive about work and so disconnected from myself and from you. The way your work was a gift to me was that I feel inspired to learn how to process my emotions, even though I am scared as hell to do it."

I turned to Thomas, "Now it's your turn to take a dose."

Thomas said, "Then, the situation is . . . I do anything I can to avoid my feelings. I want the baby, but I don't know if I can be a good father. I work all the time. I have no relief other than my easiest outlets, weed and videogames."

"What are you most stressed about, Thomas?"

"What I am most stressed about is . . . I don't know how to be a good dad. I feel ANGRY that . . . I do not know how to be a father. I CAN'T STAND IT that I had no role models for being anything other being a real jerk. I HATE it that . . . I DO NOT KNOW what I'm DOING! I really fucking HATE that! I am fucking furious that . . . I could turn into a really bad father like my dad. I hate that! I FUCKING HATE THAT!!!!"

"Brilliant! Stay with anger until sadness comes."

He continued, "I feel sad that . . . I don't know what I am doing. I feel afraid that . . . I will become a dad, then do it wrong. I feel guilty that . . . I hide behind weed and videogames. I feel grateful that . . . I am owning up to this and not ducking out. I feel happy that . . . I have such a beautiful wife. I feel secure that . . . I will do whatever I can to learn how to be a good dad . . . and I feel proud that . . . I am expressing my feelings."

"Great work, Thomas! Fantastic!"

He launched right into the next lead-in, "I want to do the take action part . . . I expect myself to do the best I can to . . . raise our baby differently than I was raised. My positive, powerful thought . . . I CAN DO THAT! The essential pain? I must give at a deeper level. I can't just turn my mind off and escape. I can't be an addict. I can't be like my dad. My earned reward is . . . freedom. I want freedom from being like my father. I want freedom from all the common excesses."

I said, "Take a deep breath, Thomas, and enjoy this moment!"

"I am . . . I'm at One, I feel victorious and . . . great!"

"You're about to be a dad and you have tools so that you can change your wiring, not by chance but by choice. You're already doing it, and the stronger your pathways of radical resilience are, the easier it will be to pass them along to your child."

He said, "I want our baby to be Wired at One and have all the joys of a purposeful life. Nothing is more important than that, not weed, videogames, or work. Nothing else even comes close."

I said, "Gretchen, would you like to give Thomas a connecting message?"

She said, "Thomas, when you did your work, the feelings and sensations in my body were . . . tenderness and love. The way your work was a gift to me was . . . I realize that I've been yelling at you a lot, and it's not all your fault. I've been emotionally shut down. And I shouldn't be drinking, either."

Thomas said, "I know it's hard. I love you, Gretchen."

Gretchen and Thomas had time before the baby was born to strengthen their resiliency pathways. Pregnancy is stressful, so the prenatal work they were doing would be more likely to be encoded in their long-term memory systems. They could learn the techniques together during pregnancy and in the years to come.

Yet, at that moment, after they had both spiraled up to One, love was in the air. It was magical – for Thomas and Gretchen, for me – and I believe it was magical for their baby . . .

Chapter 9.

Keep it Simple: The 3 Rules

When the entire world is shaken by a pandemic, which then spawns more chaos, harm, and revolutions, it is a profound moment of opportunity. Stress levels are so high that the unconscious mind is wide open – the synaptic connections between neurons fluid – offering us a biological invitation for transformation.

The neuroscience has shown us that during stressful times we can boost our power if we pause and turn our attention away from the busy thoughts of our neocortex and toward the wisdom of our body. Then, if we connect to the deepest part of ourselves and process our emotions, we can update our emotional architecture and open up new and better possibilities in our lives.

By reading this book, you have explored this new "body part" of the emotional brain and entered into the process of learning how to work with it to improve the quality of your life. However, there are some big ideas to extract from this book, three in particular. Let's look at them.

Rule #1
Focus on Process, Not Outcome

If we get the process right, the outcome takes care of itself. This is easier said than done because we can see the outcome. We lost ten pounds, we filed our taxes on time, we took out the trash. It's so satisfying. It gives us the illusion of control.

When we happen to get the brain process right, we're rewarded, more often than not, in exceeding our expectations about the outcome. Magic happens, and we predictably follow through in a state of connection (after the various Brain States 4 and 5 along the way) and higher purpose.

We must give up on the idea that what matters is the outcome. That is definitely true if a baby is crying, a friend is in dire straits, or a car is about to sideswipe us. But our stressed brains tend to generalize these rare threats to just about everything, creating so much urgency to perform that our inner process seems of no importance.

Quite a while back, I wrote a grant to teach stress techniques and healthy nutrition in a largely African American community in Marin County. I pushed myself past any reasonable limits, but made the grant deadline and was elated. I know I wasn't as available to my three children as I needed to be during that time. Six weeks later, I was notified that the grant was turned down. I remember going to pick up one of my children from their summer day camp and sobbing in the car.

Now I ask myself, "Why?" When I had started out writing the grant, I was at Brain State 1, charged up and happy that we could help this community. With our research team, we visited the health education center, collaborated with community leaders, and believed that we could help out. Grant writing can be intense, along with all the pressures of life, and along the way, my devil of a reptilian brain took over. I put meeting the grant deadline ahead of some of my more meaningful and true needs. I pushed myself way too hard and my Brain State 1 made the infamous 1-to-5 flip.

I had started off running resilient wires that were so strong that I was at One most of the time. At some point, I must have taken my fingers off the pulse of my inner life, and stopped putting process before outcome. I no longer was attaching to authenticity, that I had three children who needed a lot of attention, and integrity, that it wasn't right for me to ignore my health and their needs on the chance that some grant, even a worthy one, could be funded. Instead, I attached to something else, perhaps the false high of stress overload or the image of myself being a savior. Perhaps it was that I needed the funding to support my family. That figured in, too.

As Brain States 1 and 5 are the only reward states, and the brain is driven both to reduce threats to support survival and to be rewarded, these two states can easily trade places. Each is an imposter of the other. Perhaps this is a neuroscience application of the higher you go, the harder you fall, but even when we are doing things for all the right reasons, the reward chemicals can trick us.

It's sometimes hard to differentiate between the body feel of Brain State 1, a natural sustainable high, and the body feel of Brain State 5, an addictive, crash-and-burn high of stress overload. The only chance we have to learn it and to protect ourselves from stress overload is to honor the primacy of process over outcome.

The emotional brain in disconnection and stress is our nemesis, and in connection and joy it is our best friend, or so it seems. Perhaps the reality that Brain State 5 resides inside us, always waiting in the wings, a nanosecond away from a reactive wire being triggered and calling it to center stage, is yet another gift of the universe. It might be.

Only at Brain State 5 do the circuits that cause extremes, suffering, addiction, and despair unlock. If we somehow muster enough self-regulatory strength from the prefrontal cortex to stay emotionally aware, the circuits can change. In that moment, if we do not stay connected to ourselves, the old circuits take over. We go to 5. Then the drama heats up. Will we reconnect to our feelings or allow the reptilian brain to have its way with us?

This is the gritty, dynamic, high-conflict world of our emotional brain. Nobody wants to feel so overloaded, but what would life be like if we did not have these moments of struggles, temptations, and battles? Those reactive circuits would continue to live in our emotional brain, firing, wiring, becoming stronger, and causing more suffering until they finally get our attention, making us feel bad enough that we dig a little deeper. If instead, we go into Brain State 5 with more resolve, we can stay connected to the deepest part of ourselves, burrow through our toxic emotions, and sometimes spiral up to a state of connection that warms our hearts. We have tested ourselves and discovered that we actually are worthy, we are not bad, we do have power, and we can have joy.

Honoring the primacy of process gives us an internal way of protecting ourselves against the stress of the world and relief from the unprocessed stress that has wormed its way into our inner life.

One way to help make that switch to putting process first is to develop a personal phrase that gives you a reminder. Any words that convey the idea of getting to One first, before focusing on the outcome, can help. It's most useful if it is short and fun to say. Humor helps, too. Some examples are: "Process before outcome," "Am I at One?" and "Connect inside, not with people, places, or things."

Rule #2
See Life as a Joy Response

For those new to the EBT, one of the first annoyances of using it is all this "joy" stuff. It can be so irritating.

Joy is perhaps the most important word in the method because of its neuroscience roots. Neuroscientist Antonio Damasio wrote in *Looking for Spinoza: Joy, Sorrow, and the Feeling Brain:* "Joyous states signify optimal physiological coordination and the smooth workings of the operations of life."

With those words, Damasio dealt a deathblow to our conventional thoughts about physiology. Homeostasis used to be bland. It was the internal processes seeking to create balance. We didn't have to feel rewarded. Being calm, composed, and even-tempered was enough.

George Vaillant furthered that premise in his work, *Spiritual Evolution*, showing the biological basis and need for the joyous, elevated emotions. This mirrors neurobiological attachment science, which shows that a mother connects with her crying baby in a progression of emotions, culminating in shared joy.

For decades, we thought of homeostasis as being the fundamental process of life. Every high school junior learned the word, and it was core to biology. Our genes evolved to balance our physiology, everything from our heart rate and blood pressure to our body temperature. When allostasis was discovered in 1988, it was clear that this toxic stress state made stress bad for us. We couldn't clear our toxic emotions, so we had to wait for the stress to dissipate.

The allostatic response's strength is so formidable that it shaped how we think about the entire stress response. If a strong reactive wire is triggered, we lose control. There is no nice, sweet spiraling up to joy. We're completely stuck.

For example, when I was co-directing the adolescent eating disorder clinic at the University two decades ago, we treated young people with bulimia. A stress-reactive survival circuit was the problem, but one day a teenager, Charlotte, explained to me why she was out of control with her eating.

She said, "Once I start, it's not that I *won't* stop. I *can't* stop. Only when the entire carton of ice cream is gone or the dry cake mix box is emptied or if my mom or dad comes home unexpectedly can I stop. It's only when something outside me makes me stop or that I can't physically eat any more."

These circuits can be that strong. However, times have changed and so has the science. If I were treating Charlotte today, she would learn how to rewire a really strong "bulimia" circuit, which involves a slightly different use of the dose. In addition, she'd learn how to make connections with others and use the tools or take several doses to switch off that wire. She would not have to do this perfectly, but in time, she would learn that she had control over her emotions and her drives. Her stress buzzer wouldn't have to stay stuck on. She would have the power to exert more control over her moments of toxic stress.

That's what we see today in program participants, whether the triggered wire leads to eating disorders, stuck moods, relationship meltdowns, or productivity problems. The stress buzzer does not have to become stuck on. They can switch it off by embracing EBT as a first-response strategy, a way to use their natural powers to resolve issues and access joy.

Recently, I began wondering, if we could switch off stress, and that switch led to joy, why we didn't update our thinking about the stress response, seeing it as the joy response. Our physiology yearns to move through any stress back to joy, as that joy state is optimal for the survival of the species. With a new capacity to bounce back faster, the arousal of a stress response could be followed by a drive for joy.

With our reset of how we process emotions, when we feel triggered, we are stressed out in the moment, but, in truth, we are on our way back to joy. We're having a bit of an emotional cleanse, clearing out some stress clutter, and updating a few errant circuits, but we're on our way!

Now that we can move through all emotional states relatively rapidly, we can see the stress response as the joy response. We're always on the pathway back to joy. In introducing this concept in my telegroups, the response was enthusiastic, and they applied it immediately.

A trial attorney who was in the group shared, "I had a stalled situation with my wife, and I was shutting down. As soon as she starts criticizing me, I go right to Brain State 5. I emotionally vacate the situation. Yesterday when I went into my stalled state with her, I reminded myself that I wasn't in toxic stress, but in a state of 'pre-joy.' That was enough for me to come out of emotional hiding, and our conversation began to flow again."

Another participant, Janey, was working on a circuit triggered in her work environment. Her boss, who reminded Janey of her mother, would favor her co-worker, triggering Janey's childhood wires. She said, "To get at these wires, I've been at 5 for a few days. They are gnarly circuits. When at 5, I know I am alive, and on my way to a burst of joy!"

What's a personal phrase that will guide you to see stress as part of the larger arc of physiology that is taking you to joy? Try out some brief ones and don't hold back on humor or the adroit use of expletives. The brain hears them! Two examples are: "This is pre-joy. I'm on my way!" or "After the stress comes the joy – Fantastic!"

Rule #3
Know Your Earned Reward

This is by far the easiest rule of the three. Each time you give yourself a dose of EBT, you experience one of the earned rewards of a purposeful life. The reward center shines, you feel ripples of pleasure in your body, and you go forward and do things you did not want to do. It doesn't matter if it is scrubbing the kitchen floor, soothing a disgruntled customer, or going for a walk around the block rather than using the calming impact of eating sweets. You can do it and it is effortless, even fun.

Now that you know the process, you can get to purpose most of the time, and not by chance, but by taking those precious four-minute breaks and spiraling up. Sometimes you'll need someone to listen to you or it will take several doses to get to purpose, but you can do that.

The rule is that when we go forward fueled by the chemical surges activated by radical resilience, we are reaping the benefits of higher-order rewards. Our evolutionary biology rewards us chemically when we go forward with the greater good in mind, and we are in a new mindset. Life becomes easier, we don't judge our Brain State 5 moments, as we are not only on our way to joy, but to purpose.

Moments of magic big and small come into normal daily life, and some of the bigger hurdles we face, though still challenging, we can somehow get over.

For example, for a long stretch of time, I was a single parent, while taking care of my own parents who were both elderly and not well, and transitioning my children into adulthood. Dating was not my highest priority. Yet I knew on a body level that if I went to my deathbed without at least trying to find love, I would disappoint myself and, in my way of thinking at the time, not model for my children the art and science of being fearless. The reward that came to mind was intimacy. That was logical. Soon after that I met Walt, who is now my husband. I still believed my reward was intimacy until the relationship heated up and my lizard brain decided to present me with some of the reactive wires encoded from childhood hurts and later relationship foibles.

On my way to a date with Walt, I was driving along the hilly streets of San Francisco giving myself dose after dose. I was running at Brain State 4.8, which was just what I needed to know the deepest part of myself.

I had my expectation, which was to do my best to connect with myself and give this man love, stopping short of abusing or neglecting myself. I fully anticipated that the reward that would arrive in my mind from that deep, primitive place in my emotional brain would be intimacy. Then it appeared. My reward was spirituality.

In that moment, I understood. It looked like this adventure was about loving this man, but in the depth of the threat of getting close were all its vulnerabilities and essential pains – he could reject me, I could waste a lot of time, I could desert my work, and he could judge me once he really knew me. These essential pains revealed the reward of spirituality, the very same reward that nourished me at other important junctures in my life. My defining reward had been spirituality all along, and now in a completely novel and rather frightening situation, it was circling back around to nurture me through this juncture and bring into focus the coherence of my life.

That capacity to be present to our very essence, not having to guess who we are, can be life-changing. Having fresh evidence from our unconscious mind that is free of the revisions made by thoughts helps us know and love ourselves. It gives us the clarity to say, "I get it, that's what my life is about!" That becomes another magical moment, the gift of our emotional brain.

What's a good way to focus more on purpose? Say to yourself a few words, such as "What's my reward?" throughout the day. If what you are doing or about to do is of higher purpose – sanctuary, authenticity, vibrancy, integrity, intimacy, spirituality, or freedom – you are running a resilient circuit. Excellent. If not, give yourself a dose or two, and once you know your purpose, you will be unstoppable.

In becoming really comfortable as the owner and operator of your emotional brain, what do you do? You focus on the process, not the outcome. You lean into stress knowing that after the stress comes the joy. And you peer into your heart to find the rewards of purpose that matter most to you.

That's the pathway to opening yourself to living a new – and quite magnificent – life . . .

Chapter 10.

Imagine a World at One

The Covid pandemic began when a highly contagious and virulent germ was transmitted from an animal to humans. Yet the brain in toxic stress fanned the flames of spreading the virus and increased the extent of its impact. It seemed to be the worst of times, but, given that stress amplifies the plasticity of the human brain, the pandemic may have been just what we needed – a catalyst for creating a new world of hope, love, and joy.

In early 2020, we responded to the threat posed by the pandemic based on the way we saw life at that time. We launched a major offensive to protect the physical health of our communities and prevent the virus from overwhelming our healthcare system. We acted immediately to ensure food security by strengthening the crippled supply chain. We manufactured ventilators, produced personal protective equipment (PPE), and ordered sheltering in place and school closures. We set about developing a vaccine for Covid.

Yet in the midst of this massive response to protect our physical health and security, we forgot about our most valuable asset – the human brain.

During the 50 years before the pandemic, the sciences of neuroplasticity, stress physiology, and emotion regulation changed radically. We came to understand all three in vastly new and tremendously promising ways. In other areas of our response to the pandemic, we had rushed to update our approaches based on the latest science. However, the science that could have given us more power to protect our citizens from toxic stress and bring us on-the-spot resiliency was ignored. We are now paying a horrendous price for that omission, which shows up in frightening increases in health problems and puts us on a trajectory that could cripple our recovery and amplify our suffering.

It's time to come to terms with the reality that our approach to stress, however well-intentioned, is broken. It treats our stress as homeostatic, whereas we are experiencing the more toxic, allostatic stress levels. The current stress-reduction strategies of healthy lifestyle, social support, and positive thinking rely on exceptional cognitive functioning. When we are in stress, the thinking brain relinquishes personal control to the reflexive responses of the emotional brain. We repeat old, unhealthy patterns. Then, we blame ourselves and ask, "Why do I keep doing that?" We do it because cognitive control is not enough to switch out of toxic stress. We need a stress solution. Our current methods were perfect for the 1950s, workable in the 1990s, but have failed us in 2020.

We can recover from our foibles with stress, and perhaps this is just as it should be. All of us were in stress when the threat of the coronavirus appeared in our lives.

We did what we could do at the time, but now we must make stress a priority. We need a significant reset, a vaccine of sorts, high-octane resiliency tools that give us internal protection against toxic stress. Just how people someday will be exposed to the coronavirus but not become infected with it after getting the vaccine, the new approach to stress must enable us to be exposed to a stressed-out world without being infected with toxic stress.

Our pathway to stress protection is radical resiliency, which uses the power of our own emotions. Emotional processing can strengthen brain circuits that detoxify negative, stress-charged emotions. It can clear away the stress and transform these emotions into elevated feelings such as love, compassion, gratitude, hope, forgiveness, awe, and joy. Science has shown that we cannot think our way through stressed-out states to these elevated states of being. To heal ourselves, we must feel, not the way we did in pre-Covid times, but instead increasing the sophistication of our approach to reflect the latest science.

We can do that because the brain pathways of radical resiliency are very precise, and the process is reproducible. In a way, it mirrors what our hunter-gatherer ancestors did to work through their worries. We begin by complaining about what is bothering us. The stress center (the amygdala) awakens the reactive wires stored in the unconscious mind and unlocks their synaptic connections. At that moment, we rapidly release our stress with a brief expression of healthy anger, which quickly resets the prefrontal cortex to process our remaining emotions with symphonic precision. Our emotions flow from negative to positive. We do not stay in our bliss. Instead, we are grounded in reality and recognize our need to be productive. We bring to mind our higher purpose and a plan of action and are rewarded with surges of dopamine and endorphins. We find ourselves at a sturdy, shining Brain State 1. This entire orchestration of chemical and electrical resiliency typically takes four minutes or less.

This process of rewiring how we respond to stress was developed over a span of 40 years, with contributions from some of the most innovative minds in neuroscience and by applying the most respected emerging research. Yet, the idea of unpacking toxic emotions and turning off the spigot of stress hormones at their source – the human brain – in real-time remains novel.

The approach is an application of the science of positive emotional neuroplasticity. In 1999, a breakthrough book on emotional plasticity, *A General Theory of Love*, broke new ground in the field. The authors were three of my colleagues, Thomas Lewis, Richard Lannon, and Fari Amini, professors at the Langley Porter Psychiatric Institute. I was captivated by their book and sent them my research, one of my books on the method, and a note mentioning that the EBT tools seemed to be rewiring the emotional brain.

I didn't hear from them for two weeks.

Then, late one afternoon, I received a phone call from Fari Amini, the senior faculty member of the three.

With a commanding voice, he asked, "Where do you live?"

I told him my home address.

Then he said, "You have discovered a public health way to rewire the emotional brain. You could live anywhere on the planet, but you live one mile from me."

We both laughed . . . and then I shivered.

That was 20 years ago.

I didn't appreciate at the time that we would need a perfect trifecta for this approach to reach its potential to become like a stress vaccine, which would be eagerly anticipated and widely distributed. First, it would take a dedicated team of neuroscientists, technologists, health leaders, and psychotherapists to sharpen the tools and whittle down the time needed to switch off stress activations. Second, it would require neuroplasticity, stress physiology, and emotion regulation science to advance, providing us with new ways to enhance the method's effectiveness. Last, we would need a shared experience of stress overload with its serious consequences, such as we have now, to appreciate the importance of updating our approach to stress.

The new approach asks us to become comfortable with taking charge of our emotional brain. It is no longer owned by psychologists, psychiatrists, and physicians. We own it. We know how it likes to process emotions and we know how to play by its rules. Gone are the days when we rely on identifying our feelings to reduce toxic stress. Now we process them, clearing away that stress and turning those negative emotions into positive ones.

In the past, we listed all our issues, from anxiety and depression to overeating and addiction. They were our problems. Now we see them for what they are: symptoms of not having had a sufficiency of skill to turn stuck emotions into feelings that flow. And what about our attitude toward stress? We lean into stress, and when it comes our way, we know it's a moment of opportunity to transform our neural pathways. Also, the previously-locked coffers of our outdated, faulty expectations and unhealed hurts are now open. We can update these wires to stop our suffering and enhance our resiliency.

As we connect with the deepest part of ourselves, more of our needs are met quite naturally. We find so much comfort, safety, and love within that we are more self-reliant. We need less from the modern world, the world that is at odds with our hunter-gather brain that prefers sameness, connection, and natural pleasures. Rather than looking to organizations – government, religions, corporations – to save us, we find that we can save ourselves. We may need them, but not too much. What saves us is our commitment to the most fundamental aspect of our lives, the processing of our emotions to clear stress and return to purpose. That process – whoosh! – brings us an astonishing new level of peace and power from within. We attach not to people, places, and things, but to life's higher-order rewards, which are sanctuary, authenticity, vibrancy, integrity, intimacy, spirituality, and freedom.

By putting process before outcome, maintaining an image in our minds of the joy response, and finding a higher purpose, we change chemically and electrically. We realize that we have discovered the missing link that enables us to live in the modern world without surrendering to it. We adopt a more vibrant lifestyle, such as eating home-cooked meals, playing music, singing songs, or planting a garden. Our senses come alive and our creativity blossoms. We are so much happier that we might even find ourselves humming. Life is very good and very right.

Our health improves. As most health problems are caused or exacerbated by stress, with less stress, we are apt to have fewer health problems. Also, the natural healing chemicals of optimal physiology encourage the body to heal itself. We access all the healthcare we need but may discover that we need less of it. As our epidemics of anxiety, depression, obesity, and addiction are rooted in allostasis, some of our health issues may improve on their own. Our traditional treatments, when coupled with EBT, may become more effective.

Our attitudes may shift. We may become involved in changing the larger world, such as forwarding new laws. Yet we sense that laws are probably not the solution we need most. The human brain in stress finds ways to get around most of them. Even if we solve one problem, if we do not clear away the stress that fuels it, another problem will take its place. We sense that the human brain at One is the solution, and that only involves using simple emotional techniques. We can use them alone, but when two or more people gather to use them, that connection can be even more profound.

Part of this shift in attitudes is toward the planet. Climate change, flooding, fires, as well as the encroachment on wildlife habitat – which promote animal viruses crossing over to humans – all begin to bother us more. We are so present to our emotions and sensations that we actively decide how we can help Mother Earth and do our part.

Where do we begin? Start by seeing the simplicity of how emotions flow in a very logical way, and that feelings are not beyond our control but our pathway to control.

Then, appreciate that the first time you use the technique, it might feel uncomfortable to you. The reptilian brain will not be happy that you discovered this approach. It resists change. It likes stress overload and is comfortable with emotional disconnection; it has become a habit. However, soon you will win over your reptilian brain and find that you can spiral up to One with ease, and for that moment, life is astonishingly beautiful.

Last, ask yourself: What if I were not afraid to feel? What if I made friends with fury, sadness, fear, and guilt, knowing that their purpose was to make me radically different, in a new state of being? That dip into negative emotions would awaken you to your joy and to the enduring rewards in life.

Each time we release stress, we connect to the deepest part of ourselves and tap into the wisdom of one of the seven rewards of purpose. That connection sparks a desire to give to others and each act of kindness, particularly when it takes our breath away, is what really matters. Our generosity of spirit becomes part of others, and a way in which we become everlasting.

So, what is the ultimate message? Do not be afraid to feel. We have a beautiful brain. It is the gift from our genes, a loving God, or both. Emotions do flow through it – we can turn even the most harmful emotions into healing feelings like love, forgiveness, and hope. Our choice to be fearless and lean into our gritty feelings unlocks the portals of our emotional brain. What arrives? Exquisite moments of spiritual evolution and lightness of being. That is joy!

As the emotional brain is the center of imagination, we can use it to help us out in another way. What we choose to imagine becomes a neural network, and neural networks create our new reality.

If you will, please join me in imagining walking through your day with the stress of the world coming into your brain. Instead of getting stuck, that stress flows right through you, and in a matter of a few moments, you spiral up to One. Your mind settles on the reward of purpose that matters most to you at the time, and you feel the glow.

Your day continues, but now you are radiating the One state. It touches someone close to you and a sense of peace and power comes over them. They feel better, too. Your inner state of peace and power is catching.

Next, see yourself encountering a child who wonders why they feel so good when they are around you. You tell them the story of the emotional brain . . .

In a challenging time of your life, you learned of a new way of being. You learned how to stay connected to your emotions and make them flow. It was not always easy, but you connected to the deepest part of yourself, and you found magic there – and a desire to give back. Then, you gave back, and by giving back, you felt complete.

The child listens and learns.

Last, see that warm connection inside you radiating outward. The world remains conflicted, tormented, and extreme, but now the magic of the emotional brain seems to be catching on. More people are beginning to feel compassion for themselves, compassion for others, and compassion for all living beings. The planet matters, all people matter, injustice matters, and there is a new excitement about all the things we need to do to make the world a better place.

You have done your small but important part to be at One, and from that choice, one person after another, and another is inspired to be at One. Pause for a moment until you see . . . that out of the ashes of the pandemic, in our own messy and imperfect way, we have changed. We are connected to ourselves and to others and are moving forward in life. We are a World at One.

If you can imagine that, it could happen . . .

Epilogue:
A Revolution From Within

As of this writing, the pandemic appears to have opened us to extreme opportunities for transformation. These transitional times in human history come for a good reason. When the world has changed significantly, and the human spirit cannot accept life as it is anymore, some revolution erupts. Often, a gush of overdue awakenings follows. We have periods of transition, typically every 60 to 100 years, and this may be what we are experiencing now.

We are in the midst of widespread change. During another time of change, as a fresh-faced student at Berkeley, I recall walking through Sather Gate in a haze of tear gas. There were placards and sit-in signs everywhere. Much of the protesting was against the Vietnam War, but also represented were the free speech movement, plus social change around gay rights, civil rights, and zero population growth (which did not catch on). Feminist groups held workshops for discovering sexual rapture, bands of students moved along Piedmont Avenue high on LSD, and we were all inspired to rally around ecology by Rachael Carson's *A Silent Spring*. There was violence, anger, fear, and possibility.

We believed that we were on the precipice of creating a new world, and all our attention was on the social movements, without understanding how to shore up our emotional brain to process it all and minimize our suffering. I believe we are on that precipice again now, except we have a far more expansive opportunity to set a new course to make a new and better world. Although there are many revolutions and changes in the works, we know that the first revolution is within ourselves.

We have all the brain function we need to create that internal shift. According to Harvard professor George Vaillant, evolution has made us spiritual creatures, and over time, we are destined to become more so. Our brain is the product of three evolutions, a natural selection of genes that moved us from reptiles to *Homo sapiens*, which was followed by a cultural evolution that led us through language development and sharing, not only to survive but to thrive. Last, we evolve over our lifespan that leads us from the moment of recognition of our existence to such heights of resilience that altruism reigns and we feel joy in giving back. These three evolutions of the brain linked our reward center and our center for higher purpose, so we can clear our stress and bring to mind our higher purpose and feel vibrant.

As you create that revolution from within, you will see the world differently. You will think in terms of wires – reactive or resilient – or, if you prefer, brain states. Be gentle with yourself. Begin by asking yourself, "Do I want to get to One?" and if you do not, then stay in your current brain state. You have that right!

However, more and more, you'll say, "Why not take a few minutes, and strengthen my resiliency pathway? I can do it while I'm watering my herb garden, cooking that healthy dinner, or going for a walk with my mask on." Start living in the world of your emotional brain and notice how relaxed you are.

When you are ready to use the tools, use them alone. A great way to start is to read the stories in this book, and you'll probably find yourself saying the lead-ins to yourself. When it sounds like fun, try out the technique when you are stressed. See how well it works, and notice if you have any missing feelings. A missing feeling is one emotion your brain cannot find easily. That's important information because if any of the eight emotions of the technique is missing, the emotional flow shuts down.

Notice that as you use the lead-in for that missing emotion, that emotion becomes stronger. It becomes an emotional muscle that you build up, and your emotions flow much more easily. Each time you use the technique and your emotions flow, you strengthen your pathways of radical resilience, and over time, your brain becomes your internal protection against stress overload. Situations that used to trigger you don't anymore. As these circuits control your body chemistry, you notice how much healthier you feel, and it's all because you decided to step through the portal of your emotional brain and become a fully vibrant emotional being.

Before long, someone will notice that your energy has changed and ask what have you been doing for yourself. Have you found new love or perhaps experienced a spiritual awakening? I have found that the pathway to transmitting the work can be very indirect. You share that you are using the stress vaccine, and it is working for you. The emotional brain has no walls, so they can feel your resilience busting through their thinking brain and it feels so good to be with you. They want what you have.

If you like, invite someone to be your connection buddy, someone who listens to you get from stress to joy and says some kind words to you. Do the same for them, too. Notice how safe that feels and that you're happier, more resourceful, and enjoying the connection. Even having one person as a connection buddy can make a world of difference.

This is one way to discover how much alike we are. If you use the tools with other people, you'll find that we all have the same feelings. Everyone else goes to Brain State 5, too, and instead of judging that state, if others understand the science of the emotional brain, they'll join you in celebrating it. Keep the process fun, as we are dealing with the reptilian brain and there is a lot to laugh about in our relationship with our inner lizard.

In a recent telegroup, there were always people in all of the brain states in any one session. If they had been alone and not understanding the science of the emotional brain, they would have been hostile, numb, depressed, or anxious. Instead, I asked for some creativity, and said, "Who wants to make up a song about Brain State 5?" One woman, who writes children's books said, "When I'm at 5, I'm alive!" Another, a nutritionist, spoke up, and said, "I can sing that!" and before long, she had the entire group of six people laughing and singing.

The stress vaccine takes us to deep levels of healing, and stress opens us to experiencing joy. In the past, we did not know how to process emotions, but that does not have to be our world anymore. We have choices. We can stop being so serious about our emotions. They are the "steam" that comes off our brain's gorgeous emotional circuitry, and we can play with our emotions and in doing so transform our lives. Emotions are no longer scattered, stuck, or toxic. They are pathways to move to One. We can do the little dance of EBT and clear away emotional clutter and discover a new zest for life!

Although EBT is designed to be fun, it is also the next step in our cultural evolution. We have the opportunity to evolve rapidly, and we're not sure how rapidly that can be. It depends upon the dose of the vaccine we take, how quickly or slowly we want to transform. Kathleen, a psychologist who used EBT, said, "I see EBT as personal development on Miracle-Gro."

Thank goodness we are living in a time when we have the science to help us lean into these challenges and come out the other side healthier and happier, even co-creators of a new world. The pathway to this moment is perfect, as we have already crossed two hurdles in human processing. One is the free speech movement, a major accomplishment from the 1960s, and the other is the ability to access information, a product of the internet and the smartphone. Right now, we have the power to speak and access information, and all we need is a way to process our freedom and information through our pathways of radical resilience. If we create that revolution from within, what will we experience? A new way to become wiser faster.

It is wisdom that we need most right now. In reflecting back on the tools and science of this book, the message is one of hope. We do have power. People can change. We can change. All we need is the inspiration to process our emotions and move forward with purpose.

Your life matters. You are an emotional being with astonishing powers if you use your emotions. If you do one thing: process your emotions, you will access your inherent strength, goodness, and wisdom. Your emotional brain will take care of the rest . . .

Appendices

A Quick Guide

For your own stress solution, begin by focusing on your body and being aware of its signals. The moment you begin to feel disconnected, stressed, confused, negative, or bad, appreciate that your emotional brain is doing you a favor. It's alerting you to your need to process your emotions and activate your natural radical resilience.

At first, you might find it difficult to listen to your body, but sooner than you might think, that will change. You will reach for EBT as your fundamental strategy for living your best life. The entire "whoosh" experience will become more automatic the more you use the technique. By using it, you are updating your relationship with yourself to be present, loving, connected, and powerful.

To give yourself a dose of EBT, use the lead-ins on the next page. Be prepared to be surprised. You will feel better, a sign that the harmful stress chemicals have turned off and your brain is activating healing chemicals. Your entire outlook on life and all you do will be more positive and productive.

What if the tool doesn't work very well? It's probably because you aren't stressed or you are in stress overload. There are other EBT tools for those other brain states, but for now, accept that the tools don't always have to work perfectly for you to experience important results. Focus on using this one technique and enjoying your new powers.

To make using the EBT techniques easier, download our mobile app, which provides all these lead-ins plus those for the other tools, as well as guided relaxations and progress tracking. It is called Brain Based Health by EBT, and it is available with memberships at ebt.org for both iPhone and Android. Members also have access to using the app on tablets and accessing the app's content through the internet, as well as to online workshops, e-learning, coaching, and support.

These are the lead-ins for the technique:

The Stress Solution

Release Stress

The situation is . . .

What I am most stressed about is . . .

I feel angry that . . .

I can't stand it that . . .

I hate it that . . .

I feel sad that . . .

I feel afraid that . . .

I feel guilty that . . .

I feel grateful that . . .

I feel happy that . . .

I feel secure that . . .

I feel proud that . . .

Take Action

I expect myself to do the best I can to . . .

My positive, powerful thought . . .

The essential pain is . . .

My earned reward is . . .

Feel a surge of JOY!

More Support

The emotional brain is the social brain and it lights up when we listen to others and they listen to us. Any inkling that it can connect to another sentient being and the reward center lights up. It is in joy.

The mainstay of the method is the private use of EBT. You use it quietly and alone by talking yourself through the prompts.

As you use it more, chances are you'll want to include others in your EBT practice. It's more fun, more effective, and a great way to share your emotional wealth. As your emotions flow and you spiral up, you inspire others and they inspire you.

As mentioned, you can create a circle of support in using the tools, and even having one connection buddy can vastly improve the quality of your experience. I have several buddies, including my husband, a couple of relatives, and a few friends. Sometimes when I'm facilitating an EBT telegroup and am stressed, I use the tools in the session. This practice of having a simple, structured system for personal resilience and emotional connection makes for a better quality of life. Each connection takes about five minutes. There is no chit chat and both people know the rules (see "How to Make a Connection" on the following page) and those five minutes break the toxic spiral of stress and lift our spirits.

Create your own circle of support when you are ready or access a ready-made circle of support by joining a telegroup at the EBT website. All connections are made by telephone because the emotional brain relishes the sound of the human voice. Texting and emailing do not have the same emotional impact, and video does not provide needed privacy. What follows is a quick guide to making a connection.

How to Make a Connection

Each connection is the same. One person contacts the other and asks, "Is this a good time?"

If they say yes, then they both agree on who will use the technique and who will be the listener. If they say no, the connection ends.

Both people agree to stay within the program guidelines: do not make judgments, offer no unasked-for advice, do not interrupt, be a warm presence, agree to not mention other programs or products, and keep the connections private and confidential.

One person uses the technique.

The other listens.

Then the listener says some kind words, completing these sentences:

"When you did your work, the feelings and sensations in my body were . . ." (e.g., "sad, then happy" or "relieved and tingling").

"The way your work was a gift to me was . . ." (e.g., "I learned a lot" or "I felt inspired").

Then both say good-bye.

Sample Connection

"Hi Marcie, this is Dave."

"Hi Dave."

"Is this a good time?"

"Yes."

"Do you want to use the tools?"

"Yes, I could. What about you?"

"I'd rather listen."

"Great. The situation is . . . I just went on a job interview and I expected them to offer it to me on the spot, but they didn't. I need to start working again, and it takes a long time to get an interview and this one did not work out. What I'm most stressed about is . . . I think I made a bad impression on the interviewer. I feel angry that . . . I blew it. I can't stand it that . . . they didn't like me. I HATE it that . . . I failed again. I feel sad that . . . they didn't offer me the job. I feel afraid that . . . I won't get a job. I feel guilty that . . . I get discouraged so easily. I feel grateful that . . . I had an interview. I feel happy that . . . I have friends and family. I feel secure that . . . I will get a job at some point. I feel proud that . . . I am not giving up! Okay, now to take action: I expect myself to do the best I can to . . . get a job. My positive, powerful thought . . . I have power. I can do that! The essential pain . . . it takes work. My earned reward . . . integrity. Okay, I'm at One."

"Dave, when you did your work, the feelings and sensations in my body were . . . sad, then excited. The way your work was a gift to me was . . . Sometimes I am easily discouraged, too. I feel less alone. You helped me."

"Thanks, great connection."

"Bye."

"Bye."

The emotional shift through connecting with others is amazing. In five minutes (no more than 10), both people feel renewed and share an experience of authenticity and well-being. They just use the tools and warmly say good-bye – private, confidential, and powerful.

Our research has shown that these connections increase how much people like EBT and improve their health outcomes. People helping people help themselves use these tools of radical resilience is the new self-care of our times. Making connections with others is an important way for you to contribute to creating a world at One. We are all in this beautiful-but-stressed world together and we can lend a hand in helping each other experience radical resilience – and the power to be at One.

Next Step

You may want to use this book as the totality of your EBT practice. This technique is that powerful. However, after using the technique for a while, you might want to raise your brain's set point by adding more tools to your repertoire.

The goal of the EBT program is to provide a pathway for accomplishing that. The reptilian brain resists raising our set point, and we have developed a series of courses that seeks to outsmart the reptile. It takes about a year to complete, although some people enjoy a more leisurely experience. The goal is for you to have an abundance of all seven earned rewards and a set point at One. That produces radical resilience and comfort in being in all five brain states, with the default state of the brain in homeostasis.

If you are considering learning more about EBT, ask yourself two questions and make a plan. Then visit our website at ebt.org and choose a membership option that is right for you.

1. **Which is the reward you want most right now?**
   - ☐ **Sanctuary**   **peace & power from within**
   - ☐ **Authenticity** **feeling whole & being genuine**
   - ☐ **Vibrancy**   **healthy with a zest for life**
   - ☐ **Integrity**   **doing the right thing**
   - ☐ **Intimacy**   **giving & receiving love**
   - ☐ **Spirituality**   **grace, beauty & mystery of life**
   - ☐ **Freedom**   **common excesses fade**

Keep this reward in mind as you develop your plan. If you checked more than one reward or all of them, that is fine, too.

2. In the last week, how often did you feel:

Great! (Brain State 1)

☐ 0=rarely ☐ 1=sometimes ☐ 2=often ☐ 3=very often

Good (Brain State 2)

☐ 0=rarely ☐ 1=sometimes ☐ 2=often ☐ 3=very often

A Little Stressed (Brain State 3)

☐ 3=rarely ☐ 2=sometimes ☐ 1=often ☐ 0=very often

Definitely Stressed (Brain State 4)

☐ 3=rarely ☐ 2=sometimes ☐ 1=often ☐ 0=very often

Stressed Out! (Brain State 5)

☐ 3=rarely ☐ 2=sometimes ☐ 1=often ☐ 0=very often

Total Set Point Score _____

The EBT program is the same for all people. You begin by learning how to use the tools of the method, followed by a course on how to rewire. After completing that course, move on to Advanced EBT, with one course for each of the seven rewards. All courses are designed to provide one skill per day for 30 days, taking longer than 30 days, if you like.

Calculate your set point score and identify your stress solution plan. If your stress is on the high side, you'll need more support, but the outcome remains the same: Wired at One.

Your Stress Solution Plan

Set Point Score	Plan
12 to 15	The Family and Friends Plan
8 to 11	The Learn How to Rewire Plan
0 to 7	The Healthcare Plan

The Family and Friends Plan

Your set point is high, and you will be able to move through the EBT courses rapidly. Count on using our self-study program for the courses and involving a circle of friends and family members who are also interested in raising their set point.

The Learn How to Rewire Plan

Your set point is moderate and your brain is already somewhat resilient. Use our self-study program for the courses and access support not only from family members and friends but through our community programs. There are weekly and daily telegroups as well as concierge coaching. Enjoy raising your set point and accessing all seven of the earned rewards.

The Healthcare Plan

Your set point is in stress and your reptilian brain would be happy keeping it there. Move through the EBT courses at a pace that feels comfortable to you. Be particularly gentle with yourself when you begin, as the reptile will fight back. If you take 10 doses daily for a few days, you will feel fantastic, but then the reptile will fight back and you'll be at Brain State 5 for several days. Instead, keep your sense of adventure and sense of humor as you move through the courses. Be sure to access good healthcare to address any health concerns, and join a telegroup or access coaching – or both. Stay with the program until you are Wired at One and enjoy every step of your journey.

If you are not sure which plan is right for you, set this book and the stress solution aside for now. It will be here for you and chances are, when the time is right, you will return to it. In the meantime, please share these ideas with others to help them get from stress to joy in challenging times. We are all in this together!

Glossary

A+ Anger – Healthy, productive anger that activates stress-reactive circuits to help unlock them and release enough stress to put the thinking brain back online.

Allostasis – A physiological state of stress overload that has no shut-off valves and can be ineffective and deleterious.

Allostatic Circuit – A wire that activates an ineffective stress response. Also called a stress-reactive wire.

Allostatic Load – The wear and tear on the body and brain that accumulates from repeated episodes of allostasis.

Authenticity – The second of the seven rewards of purpose. Defined as feeling whole and being genuine.

Be Positive Tool – One of the three types of Cycle Tools. Used at Brain State 4 for situational stress. The first step of the stress solution.

Brain Based Health – The health approach of using the power of the brain to improve physiology by rewiring the stress response.

Brain State – One of five physiological states of stress arousal that impacts the entire body and brain and can change rapidly.

Connecting Message – A structured, simple response after listening to someone use an EBT tool that promotes empathy and emotional connection.

Core Circuit – Generalizations of expectations, either effective or ineffective: e.g., I do have power vs. I do not have power.

Cycle Tool – The tool for Brain State 4 in the EBT 5-Point System. There are three types of Cycle tools, depending upon what is causing this level of stress.

Earned Rewards – The enduring values that motivate and reward us with sustainable surges of neurotransmitters. The EBT system has seven of them.

Emotional Brain – The limbic brain and reptilian brain, the subcortical structures of the unconscious memory system.

EBT 5-Point System – The Emotional Brain Training system of stress resilience and emotion and behavior regulation.

Essential Pain – The unavoidable hard part of life we need to accept in order to grow and change.

Freedom – The seventh of the seven rewards of purpose. Defined as common excesses fade.

Homeostasis – A physiological state of balance that has shut-off valves and can be effective and healing.

Homeostatic Circuit – A wire that activates an effective stress response. Also called a stress-resilient wire.

Integrity – The fourth of the seven rewards of purpose. Defined as doing the right thing.

Intimacy – The fifth of the seven rewards of purpose. Defined as giving and receiving love.

Limbic Brain – The brain of emotions, attachment, appetite, rewards, sexual behavior, and spiritual connection. Part of the emotional brain, the unconscious memory system.

Neocortex – The executive functioning or overseer of our responses to life, also referred to as the prefrontal cortex or thinking brain.

Neuroplasticity – The ability of the brain to change throughout life.

Prefrontal Cortex – The executive functioning or overseer of our responses to life, also referred to as the neocortex or thinking brain.

Radical Resilience – The habit of quickly and easily moving from Brain States 3, 4, and 5 to One.

Reptilian Brain – The part of the brain that controls basic functioning, such as heart rate, blood pressure, and temperature. Part of the emotional brain.

Sanctuary – The first of the seven rewards of purpose. Defined as peace and power from within.

Set Point – The most common brain state of an individual, which becomes the brain's habit and is a predictor of morbidity and mortality. The ultimate goal of EBT is to raise the set point to the optimal state of One.

Spirituality – The fifth of the seven rewards of purpose. Defined as being aware of the grace, beauty, and mystery of life.

Stress-reactive Wire – A wire that activates an ineffective stress response. Also called an allostatic circuit.

Stress-resilient Wire – A wire that activates an effective stress response. Also called a homeostatic circuit.

Stress Response – A physiological reaction that occurs in response to a real or perceived threat.

Stress Solution – Using the Be Positive and Take Action Tools to boost your emotional resilience. Also called the stress vaccine.

Survival Circuit – A stress-reactive wire that encodes a false association between a fundamental need and a response that does not meet that need. Causes cravings, overreactions, and maladaptive drives (e.g., I get my safety from alcohol).

Take Action Tool – A tool to help move forward with higher purpose. The second step of the stress solution.

Thinking Brain – The executive functioning or overseer of our responses to life, also referred to as the prefrontal cortex or neocortex.

Vibrancy – The third of the seven rewards of purpose. Defined as healthy with a zest for life.

Wired at One – An optimal set point of resiliency and an abundance of the seven rewards of purpose.

Selected Readings

What follows is a list of researchers whose body of work contributed to the conceptual basis of the method and one or more citations of their research. For each researcher, their recent books published in the popular press have been listed first.

Antonio Damasio

Damasio, A. (2003). *Looking for Spinoza: Joy, Sorrow, and the Feeling Brain.* Harcourt, Inc.

Damasio, A. & Carvalho, G.B. (2013). The nature of feelings: Evolutionary and neurobiological origins. *National Review of Neuroscience* 14:143-152.

Vincent Felitti

Felitti, V.J., Jakstis, K., Pepper, V., & Ray, A. (2010). Obesity: Problem, Solution, or Both? *The Permanente Journal* 14:24-30.

Felitti, V.J., Anda, R.F., Nordenberg, D., et al. (1998). Relationship of childhood abuse and household dysfunction to many of the leading causes of death in adults: The Adverse Childhood Experiences (ACE) Study. *American Journal of Preventive Medicine* 14:245-258.

Dacher Keltner

Keltner, D. (2009). *Born to Be Good: The Science of a Meaningful Life.* W.W. Norton.

Joseph LeDoux

LeDoux, J. (2012). Rethinking the emotional brain. *Neuron* 73:653-676.

LeDoux, J. (2012). Evolution of human emotion: A view through fear. *Progress in Brain Research* 195:431-442.

Robert Lustig

Lustig, R.H. (2017). *The Hacking of the American Mind: The Science Behind the Corporate Takeover of our Bodies and Brains.* Avery.

Mietus-Snyder M.L. & Lustig, R.H. (2008). Childhood obesity: Adrift in the "limbic triangle." *Annual Review of Medicine* 59:147-162.

Bruce McEwen

McEwen, B. (2002). *The End of Stress as We Know It.* Dana Press.

Picard, M. & McEwen, B.S. (2018). Psychological stress and mitochondria: A conceptual framework. *Psychosomatic Medicine* 80:126-140.

McEwen, B.S., & Gianaros, P.J. (2011). Stress- and allostasis-induced brain plasticity. *Annual Review of Medicine* 62:431-445.

McEwen, B.S. (2009). The brain is the central organ of stress and adaptation. *NeuroImage* 47:911-913.

Michael Merzenich

Merzenich, M. (2013). *Soft-Wired: How the New Science of Brain Plasticity Can Change Your Life.* Parnassus Publishing.

Merzenich, M.M., Van Vleet, T.M., & Nahum, M. (2014). Brain plasticity-based therapeutics. *Frontiers in Human Neuroscience* 8:385.

Mahncke, H.W., Connor, B.B., Appleman, J., Ahsanuddin, O.N., Hardy, J.L., Wood, R.A., Joyce, N.M., Boniske, T., Atkins, S.M., & Merzenich, M.M. (2006). Memory enhancement in healthy older adults using a brain plasticity-based training program: A randomized, controlled study. *Proceedings of the National Academy of Science U.S.A.* 103:12523-12528.

Igor Mitrovic

Kurtzman, L. (2014). Neurobiologist Shares Personal Journey, Life Lessons in 'Last Lecture.' *UCSF News.* www.youtube.com/watch?v=uKjvQSBaWKQ

Mitrovic, I., Fish de Peña, L., Frassetto, L.A., & Mellin, L. (2011). Rewiring the stress response: A new paradigm for health care. *Hypothesis* 9:1:e1-e5.

Mitrovic, I., Mellin, L., & Fish de Peña, L. (2008). *Emotional brain training: The neurobiology of brain retraining for promotion of adaptive behaviors and state of well-being.* pp. 1-19. Institute for Health Solutions.

Bruce Perry

Perry, B.D. & Szalavitz, M. (2006). *The Boy Who Was Raised as a Dog: And Other Stories from a Child Psychiatrist's Notebook-What Traumatized Children Can Teach Us About Loss, Love, and Healing.* Basic Books.

Perry, B.D. & Hambrick, E.P. (2008). The neurosequential model of therapeutics. *Reclaiming Children and Youth* 17:38-43.

Elizabeth Phelps

Raio, C.M., Orederu, T.A., Palazzolo, L., Shurick, A.A., & Phelps, E.A. (2013). Cognitive emotion regulation fails the stress test. *Proceedings of the Natural Academy of Sciences* 110:15139-15144.

Schiller, D., Monfils, M.H., Raio, C.M., Johnson, D.C., LeDoux, J.E., & Phelps, E.A. (2010). Preventing the return of fear in humans using reconsolidation update mechanisms. *Nature* 463:49-53.

Hartley, C.A. & Phelps, E.A. (2010). Changing fear: The neurocircuitry of emotion regulation. *Neuropsychopharmacology* 35:136-146.

Peter Sterling

Sterling, P. (2014). Homeostasis vs. allostasis: Implications for brain function and mental disorders. *Journal of the American Medical Association Psychiatry* 71:1192-3.

Sterling, P. (2004). Principles of allostasis: Optimal design, predictive regulation, pathophysiology, and rational therapeutics. In J. Schulkin (Ed.), *Allostasis, Homeostasis, and the Costs of Physiological Adaptation* (pp. 17-64). Cambridge University Press.

George Vaillant

Vaillant, G. (2008). *Spiritual Evolution: How We Are Wired for Faith, Hope, and Love*. Broadway Books.

Acknowledgments

This book reflects the contributions of many people over many years. Igor Mitrovic, our scientific director, a neuroscientist, and a professor of physiology, Lynda Frassetto, a clinical professor of medicine and researcher, and Lindsey Fish, an internist and EBT clinical scholar co-created many of the fundamentals of EBT.

Our core team of EBT leaders was instrumental in the writing of this book, especially Judy Zehr, a specialist in attachment theory and the EBT Director of Community Education, Michele Welling, an internist, a specialist in addiction, the EBT director of professional education, and a dedicated editor of this book, and Arinn Testa, a psychologist and the EBT director of research. Dave Ingebritsen, Robin Anderson, Barbara Gabriel, Eve Lowry, Micheline Vargas, Sylvia Cramer, Molly Reno, Deanne Hamilton, and Bill Mory all furthered this work in unique ways. Charles Irwin, Jr., with his leadership in adolescent and young adult health, made this method possible. I am grateful to Charlie, as well as to Nancie Kester and Seth Kester-Irwin, for their support.

I am grateful to Kelly McGrath, EBT's Chief Administrative Officer, who has been with the organization for more than two decades and shared her wisdom about the focus of this book, making all the difference. I am thankful to Michael McClure, the Director of Marketing and Support, whose leadership in marketing and communications has guided our progress for nearly a decade. Dev Singh has been the Chief

Technology Officer for EBT for a decade and has built the platform and mobile app that bring the magic of the tools to so many people. Andrea Singh provided important IT consultation and design ideas. Frannie Wilson is a Member Care Specialist and edited this book. Her devotion to this project and to the method have been exceptional and much needed. Chris Wilson added his expertise and support multiple times throughout the creation of this work. Jamie Holecek produced the interior of this book and coordinated the creative production team and Steven Isakson completed the cover graphics. Joe Mellin designed the EBT portal and conceived of a technology-based center for connections, groups, and community.

My husband, Walt Rose, has been the "ideation" leader in this new phase of scalable, neuroscience-based EBT. Many of the breakthroughs in concepts and approaches in this book were generated by him. My family has supported this work, and I am particularly grateful to my son Joe Mellin and his wife Megan, my son John Rosenthal, and his wife Ana, and my daughter, Haley Mellin for advising me with tenderness and clarity over the years. I'm grateful to my brother, Steve McClure, and my sister-in-law, Vivian McClure, as well as to Lisa, Sarah, Ethan, and Colleen, who have given generous support. I am thankful to Pete and Erin Rose whose kindness has supported me along the way. I am thankful for Diana Dougherty's many caring ways. I am grateful to Tom and Caroline Rose, Dan Rosenthal, Patty Robertson, Mary Croughan, Anna Spielvogel, Deidre Taylor, David Bott, Sue Carlisle, Bryant and Betsy Young, Larry Townsend,

Lynne and Bruce McDermott, Denali Wilson, and Gail and Bill Hutchinson. Mike Bell, Kathleen Wilson, Pamela Streckroat, Martha Lupe, Jack Grehan, Raymond Manzano, Janice and Ralph Echenique, Kela and Carlos Cabrales, Lindsey Novak, and Tatihana and George Morales have been generous in their support and many kindnesses.

I am indebted to the many participants who have shared their ideas about the work over the years, and who have strengthened my belief in the perfection of the emotional brain.

Made in the USA
Coppell, TX
08 November 2020